AUTHENTIC
CHRISTIAN
FREEDOM

AUTHENTIC
CHRISTIAN
FREEDOM

Deconstructing the American Gospel of Liberty

Elizabeth L. Hinson-Hasty

ORBIS BOOKS

Maryknoll, New York 10545

Founded in 1970, Orbis Books endeavors to publish works that enlighten the mind, nourish the spirit, and challenge the conscience. The publishing arm of the Maryknoll Fathers and Brothers, Orbis seeks to explore the global dimensions of the Christian faith and mission, to invite dialogue with diverse cultures and religious traditions, and to serve the cause of reconciliation and peace. The books published reflect the views of their authors and do not represent the official position of the Maryknoll Society. To learn more about Maryknoll and Orbis Books, please visit our website at www.orbisbooks.com.

Library of Congress Cataloging-in-Publication Data

Names: Hinson-Hasty, Elizabeth L., author.
Title: Authentic Christian freedom : deconstructing the American gospel of liberty / Elizabeth L. Hinson-Hasty.
Description: Maryknoll, NY : Orbis Books, [2025] | Includes bibliographical references and index. | Summary: "Examines concepts of freedom in US Christian history, society, and theology"—Provided by publisher.
Identifiers: LCCN 2024055901 (print) | LCCN 2024055902 (ebook) | ISBN 9781626986077 (trade paperback) | ISBN 9798888660621 (epub)
Subjects: LCSH: Christianity and politics—United States—History. | Christianity—United States—History. | Liberty—United States—History.
Classification: LCC BR516 .H557 2025 (print) | LCC BR516 (ebook) | DDC 261.7/20973—dc23/eng/20241206
LC record available at https://lccn.loc.gov/2024055901
LC ebook record available at https://lccn.loc.gov/2024055902

*To the Good and Creative People of
Covenant Community Church*

CONTENTS

ACKNOWLEDGMENTS

Book projects evolve over time and in conversation with a variety of different groups and people. I first began drafting chapters of this book in 2022 as I prepared keynote addresses for the Synod School of Lakes and Prairies, which was held at Buena Vista University in Storm Lake, Iowa. Members of the Presbytery of Coastal Carolina helped me to further develop my ideas when I gave the *Hattie McNair Memorial Bible Lectures* in 2023 at Laurinburg Presbyterian Church in Laurinburg, North Carolina.

Several pastors and colleagues also took the time to reflect with me on the meaning of freedom or to read carefully and comment on parts of or complete chapters in this book. There are many to thank for their wisdom and insight, including Abbie Heimach-Snipes, James Calvin Davis, Mark Douglas, Roger Gench, Joshua Morris, and David True. Some formed a reading group that helped me tremendously and met in the summer of 2024. Rubén Arjona, Mamie Broadhurst, Jimmie Hawkins, Rodney Sadler, Melanie Jones Quarles, Shea Watts, and Lerone Wilder challenged me to reflect more intentionally out of my own experiences and why a conversation about freedom matters to me personally. All of these conversation partners generated new ideas and helped me improve the manuscript.

I am especially grateful to my editor and the editorial team at Orbis Books. Thomas Hermans-Webster, acquiring editor at Orbis, is wise, creative, and offers a careful and critical editorial eye. His enthusiasm for the project inspired me to keep writing, and he clearly understood the timeliness of the book. The editorial team at Orbis is also always a joy to work with.

My family is an ever-present support to me. They tolerated long hours devoted to writing and editing even in the midst of a move from Kentucky to North Carolina. I know that was not easy. I want to offer a special word of thanks to my dad, E. Glenn Hinson. Now in his nineties, he continues to encourage me as a scholar and teacher. I accepted a call to serve at Union Presbyterian Seminary in 2023. Despite his need for some extra support at this time, my dad understands the importance of being part of a seminary community for scholars of theology to be able to strengthen and broaden their theological study. He continues to encourage me to take on new writing projects. Dad began writing about religious liberty and freedom early on in his career and sees the significance of revisiting these themes at the present time.

You never know the impact or deficiencies of your writing until someone else reads, reflects on, and discusses your work. I want to thank you for taking the time to read, reflect, and engage others in discussion about the meaning and value of freedom. I take full responsibility for any deficiencies in this text and hope that where you discover limitations in my arguments and ideas we can enter into conversation together for the sake of embracing new ways of living and being in the world.

PREFACE

Centering My Story
in the Culture Wars

WHEREAS, The Scriptures teach that women are not in public worship to assume a role of authority over men lest confusion reign in the local church (1 Cor. 14:33–36) ... Therefore, be it RESOLVED, That we not decide concerns of Christian doctrine and practice by modern cultural, sociological, and ecclesiastical trends or by emotional factors; that we remind ourselves of the dearly bought Baptist principle of the final authority of Scripture in matters of faith and conduct; and that we encourage the service of women in all aspects of church life and work other than pastoral functions and leadership roles entailing ordination.

—Southern Baptist Convention
"Resolution on Ordination
and the Role of Women in Ministry"
1984 Annual Meeting

Taking her hand, Jesus said to her, "Talitha koum," which means, "Young woman, get up."
—Mark 5:41

My husband, Lee, first encountered my mother when he was invited to dinner at my family home. She was a great cook and loved fine porcelain dishes and decorating the table with flowers. That night, she set out a bountiful spread. Then, she welcomed him to take a seat at our table and, before praying over the evening meal, she gave an announcement: "You need to know, Lee, that we have one rule in this house. We don't use the 'F' word." Lee kept a nervous smile on his face, but I could feel his sense of hesitation about what she might say next. She elaborated, "It is not a four-letter word." Her speech slowed down so that he would have enough time to take in what she was about to say—"f-u-n-d-a-m-e-n-t-a-l-i-s-t." Growing up on the front line of the culture war shapes your family life and personal intellectual, spiritual, and ethical consciousness in a distinctive way.

My father arrived as a student at Southern Baptist Theological Seminary (SBTS) in Louisville, Kentucky, in 1954. Two years later, my parents were married in St. Louis, Missouri, and then my mother moved to Louisville. My father remained at SBTS, teaching, until his conscience forced him to leave due to the fundamentalist takeover of the institution in the 1990s. Institutional change is hard, even harder when your voice is silenced and your value denied.

Several historians and filmmakers have well documented the fundamentalist takeover of the seminary and the Southern Baptist Convention. I find *Battle for the Minds*, produced by Steve Lipscomb and first released in 1996, one of the most moving. The film captures the specific impact of this ideological shift on women being educated at SBTS. In the documentary, Baptists interviewed on both sides of the fight passionately testify to their beliefs, defending their own freedom of religious expression and the meaning of academic freedom within the context of theological education. These debates and the fundamentalist transformation of other Southern Baptist institutions were more than public and institutional debates in my family home; they were deeply personal and life-changing. They meant the fragmentation of our lives through the intrusion of the media, moves across the country, life lived apart, wounds that never fully healed, and energies invested in building new Progressive Baptist institutions.

My family nearly always ignored our society's preferences for polite dinner table conversation, opting instead to focus on religious liberty, academic freedom, and politics. Throughout the culture war of the 1980s and early 1990s and the resulting institutional transformations, my father, a church historian, appealed to notions of freedom and liberty articulated by early Baptists. He predicted the threat that fundamentalism posed to Southern Baptist institutions and emphasized a theological conviction at the center of Baptist life:

> Early Baptists put [the principle of voluntarism] at the center of their statements about freedom. In the Second London Confession of 1677, they asserted that "God alone is Lord of the Conscience" and drew from that principle the conviction that God has freed the conscience from any human teachings or decrees which stand in opposition to the Word of God.[1]

"Ironically," he wrote, "the most serious threat to the principle [in the United States] has come from those who espoused it most ardently in the beginning, namely, Baptists."[2] Conservative and fundamentalist Southern Baptists spoke of freedom and liberty while at the same time arguing for

---

[1] E. Glenn Hinson, "Doing Faith Baptist Style: Voluntarism," The Baptist History and Heritage Society and the William H. Whitsitt Baptist Heritage Society online, 2001, http://www.centerforbaptiststudies.org/pamphlets/style/voluntarism.htm.

[2] Hinson, "Doing Faith Baptist Style: Voluntarism."

the rescindment of women's ordination. They advocated in the public and political forum against equal rights for LGBTQIA-identified persons and for divesting from public education, limiting women's access to reproductive health care, restrictive immigration policies, and neoliberal economic policies.

At the height of the turmoil at Southern Baptist Theological Seminary, I remember a young pastor from Texas and an alumnus arrive at our doorstep early in the afternoon before my father came home from work. We lived just a block away from the school. I answered the door, and he seemed surprised to discover that my father had a family. The pastor so radically disagreed with my father's refusal to affirm fundamentalist statements of belief that he wanted to ensure my father knew just where he was headed. He stood on the stone walkway that led to the front door amid an impressive display of magenta phlox growing that year fervently explaining to me why I needed to give my father a pamphlet that showed the "path to salvation." The pastor made it clear that more than our salvation was at stake for him in that sidewalk conversation. He was confronting me to defend the soul of Baptist institutions and the United States as a nation. I accepted the document only to hasten his departure.

The Sunday school classes in the moderate Baptist churches we attended also had us practice sword drills to demonstrate the precision of our knowledge of biblical texts. We sang songs about marching on as Christian soldiers and the freedom to surrender our lives to Jesus and immerse ourselves in the cleansing blood of the Lamb. Among moderates, the stories of Roger Williams, John Leland, and Isaac Backus center religious liberty in Baptist life, and the First Amendment to the US Constitution is attributed to their vision.

For years, I felt a sense of cognitive, existential, and

spiritual dissonance while I lived in this tension, leaving me searching for places to find my own way to freely express my faith and beliefs. I retreated from the Evangelical world and religion itself for some time, looking for personal freedom and ways to come alive. It took the authenticity of some religious friends I met in Europe to draw me back in. To them, freedom was defined in community and meant living a life that embodies self-giving love for the sake of mutuality, reciprocity, and flourishing. Ultimately, I chose to explore the meaning of religious freedom in another denomination, one that provided an entry point into the culture war through intentional conversation with Christians from a much larger communion and people of other faiths.

Early on, I retreated from the Evangelical world, avoiding engagement of any kind with Christian siblings on the conservative side and disavowing myself of any responsibility for them. However, the present moment of political and religious polarization calls me to attend to the brokenness I experienced in the past. I am called to engage the debate about freedom and liberty in church and society on the front line of the contemporary culture war, a debate that echoes so many of my personal experiences. I feel a deep need, both personally and professionally as a scholar of theology and ethics, to articulate a more self-reflective and authentic understanding of Christian freedom and to wrestle with my own sense of moral responsibility amid our social and political divisions. In these pages, I reflect on Christian notions of freedom because it is my faith tradition and social location. I do not mean to neglect or minimize the importance of other religious perspectives on freedom. In fact, I value and learn from other religious traditions. However, I want to avoid the pitfall of speaking on behalf of others and presenting unfair and incomplete generalizations about their beliefs and religious practices. My hope is that, as you read these pages and consider competing views of freedom in contemporary religious and political debates, you will feel called to do your own self-reflection and enter into a rich dialogue with others about what it means to embody authentic Christian freedom in an increasingly diverse society today.

Elizabeth L. Hinson-Hasty
Union Presbyterian Seminary
Charlotte, North Carolina
October 2024

A NOTE ABOUT THE USE OF RACIAL AND ETHNIC IDENTIFIERS IN THIS BOOK

Scholars debate whether or not racial and ethnic identifiers should be capitalized in published or other written work. The reading group who met to discuss several chapters in this book reflected on the importance of capitalizing the terms "Black" and "Brown" to place emphasis upon a shared experience of minoritization and marginalization. However, there was some disagreement about whether or not to capitalize "white." Some argued that the term white should always be lowercase to deemphasize the social privilege associated with whiteness and lift up Blackness. Others thought that consistency is important. Throughout the book, I choose to capitalize Black, Brown, and White when emphasizing the cultural, philosophical, and political significance of these racial and ethnic identifiers and, most importantly, the racism associated with White Christian nationalism. I do not capitalize white when the term is used as a general descriptor of people of European descent.

INTRODUCTION

The Problem of Freedom

Freedom makes a huge requirement of every human being. With freedom comes responsibility.
—Eleanor Roosevelt

The Lord is the Spirit, and where the Lord's Spirit is, there is freedom.
—2 Corinthians 3:17

Freedom is one of the most enduring and critical US American values. Freedom is also central to Christian identity, thought, and traditions. However, dangers accompany such a potent word. We can take for granted that people in our society and in the churches share a common understanding of what it means to be free and who or what secures our freedom. We can also fail to imagine appropriate limits for individual liberties. Different notions of freedom inform competing moral visions of our common life together in the United States. Consider widely varying defenses of freedom within the current US political context.

Alt-right groups such as the Proud Boys, anti-vaxxers, and members of anti-government militia movements, among others, espouse pro-White rhetoric, advocate to be free from any government intervention. They see themselves as the true "guardians of freedom." White Christian nationalist rioters, many identifying with the alt-right, came together on January 6, 2021, in Washington, DC's Freedom Plaza, to "stop the steal" and overturn the counting of votes cast in support of Joe Biden's presidency. Similarly, Moms for Liberty organizations advocate for "parental rights" to guide their children's education, even if it comes at the expense of inclusion, democracy, and an educated citizenry.

Political commentators suggest that, in the past, more moderate and left-leaning politicians avoided the language of freedom and centered conversations on other values, such as community. However, in the spring of 2024, President Joe Biden made defending "bedrock freedoms" central to his cause when he announced his bid for reelection.[1] Biden and his writing team modeled his 2024 State of the Union address after President Franklin Delano Roosevelt's January 6, 1941, "Four Freedoms Speech." FDR commented on the threat of Nazism to democracy worldwide and looked forward to a world founded upon the freedoms of speech and expression, to worship in one's own way, from want, and from fear. Freedom from fear meant a "worldwide reduction in armaments to such a point and in such a thorough fashion that no nation will be in a position to commit an act of physical aggression against any neighbor—anywhere in the world."[2] Roosevelt concluded this speech with the observation that "this nation has placed its faith in freedom under the guidance of God. Freedom means the supremacy of human rights everywhere."[3]

Biden drew upon Roosevelt's vision and commitments, saying, "Not since President Lincoln and the Civil War have freedom and democracy been under assault here at home

---

[1] E. J. Dionne Jr., "Biden Is Inviting Us to Talk about Freedom. We Should," *Washington Post* online, April 30, 2023, https://www.washington-post.com/opinions/2023/04/30/biden-freedom-democrats-republicans/.

[2] "F.D.R. and the Four Freedoms Speech," FDR Library online, January 6, 1941, https://www.fdrlibrary.org/four-freedoms.

[3] "F.D.R. and the Four Freedoms Speech."

as they are today."[4] After Biden withdrew his candidacy in the summer of 2024, Vice President Kamala Harris called for freedom over chaos as she launched her campaign. "What kind of country do we want to live in?" she asked. "There are some people who think we should be a country of chaos, of fear, of hate, but us? We choose something different. We choose freedom—the freedom not just to get by but get ahead, the freedom to be safe from gun violence, the freedom to make decisions about your own body."[5] Harris instituted several freedom tours targeting different audiences across the nation. The "Fight for Our Freedoms College Tour" asked students to join together to work on issues that disproportionately affect young people, including reproductive freedom, gun safety, climate action, voting rights, LGBTQ+ equality, and book bans.

A Critical Moment for Church and Society

I could provide other examples, but these few stories illustrate how competing ideas of freedom reflect palpable and real tension and conflict in the United States. The story of the culture war is often told as one with two sides. One side of the debate draws on the value of freedom, especially religious freedom, which was originally intended to create the context for diverse and free expressions of faith, and turns it into a tool to impose conservative White Christian beliefs and values. The other side fights back by arguing for concepts of freedom grounded in separative individualism that too frequently fail to incorporate a deeper understanding of the essential relatedness of diverse peoples to the

---

[4] Joe Biden, "State of the Union Address, March 7, 2024," White House online, 2024, https://www.whitehouse.gov/state-of-the-union-2024/.

[5] Helen Sullivan, "We Choose Freedom': Kamala Harris Campaign Launches First Ad," *The Guardian* (July 25, 2024), https://www.theguardian.com/us-news/article/2024/jul/25/we-choose-freedom-kamala-harris-campaign-launches-first-ad.

planet Earth, our home. Politicians, religious leaders, and social activists agree that we have reached a critical moment in US history.

Today, "political polarization is the defining feature of early 21st century American politics. . . . Republicans and Democrats are further apart ideologically than at any point in recent history."[6] Leaders of both parties appeal to Christian voters in differing ways and compete "over which party is the true defender of freedom in American life."[7] Additionally, research shows that people in the United States "report a significant amount of politicking from the pulpit." It is not just occurring in churches associated with White Christian nationalist beliefs that are pressing a conservative social agenda. Across denominations, "moral issues such as abortion and prayer in schools are being raised in church almost as often as traditional issues of conscience such as hunger and poverty."[8]

Political polarization contributes to the fragmentation of congregations and denominations. Lifeway Research, an Evangelical research organization, found that "Half of US Protestants (50%) say they prefer to attend a church where people share their views on politics."[9] Ethnicity and education are also factors warranting consideration. Latinx (25%) churchgoers are far less likely to want a church with shared values than those who identify as white (54%) or

---

[6]Carroll Doherty, "7 Things to Know about Polarization in America," *Pew Research* online, June 12, 2014, https://www.pewresearch.org/short-reads/2014/06/12/7-things-to-know-about-polarization-in-america/.

[7]"'Freedom' Is America's Latest Political Football," *The Economist* online, February 23, 2023, https://www.economist.com/united-states/2023/02/23/freedom-is-americas-latest-political-football.

[8]"The Diminishing Divide . . . American Churches, American Politics," Pew Research Center online, June 25, 1996, https://www.pewresearch.org/politics/1996/06/25/the-diminishing-divide-american-churches-american-politics/.

[9]Aaron Earls, "Churchgoers Increasingly Prefer a Congregation That Shares Their Politics," Lifeway Research online, November 1, 2022.

African American (53%). Residents with less than a high
school education are less likely to be concerned that other
church members share the same political views.

Churches felt the impact of political polarization within
and between denominations and congregations as their
numbers were diminishing. Sociological studies show that
the ranks of those no longer affiliated with a religion increased until about 2016.[10] These shifts and moves from
white Evangelical to mainline denominations in more recent
years are due to either exclusivist or presumably neutral
stances taken by many faith communities regarding sexuality, sexual orientation, and transgender rights. As a result,
the unaffiliated is "one of the largest 'religious' categories
in the United States, rivaling evangelical Protestants (25%)
and Catholics (21%) and larger mainline Protestants (15%)
and those of other faiths (6%)."[11]

In this social atmosphere, we are losing the art of being
able to talk across religious, social, economic, and political differences. Many voices remain unheard, particularly
those who have the least freedom to exercise control over
their own lives. The potential for escalating the tension
and conflict that we are experiencing is real. In testimony
given on March 31, 2022, before the Select Committee to
Investigate the January 6th Attack on the United States
Capitol, Rachel Kleinfeld, a senior fellow in the Carnegie
Endowment for International Peace, Democracy, Conflict,
and Governance Program, gave witness to the fact that the
"acceptance of political violence has been rising sharply"
in recent years.[12] Threats against members of Congress

---

[10]Diana Butler Bass, "Not Dead Yet: White Mainline Protestants Now
Outnumber White Evangelicals, and Conventional Wisdom Goes Out the
Window," *The Cottage* blog, July 9, 2021, https://dianabutlerbass.substack.
com/p/not-dead-yet.

[11]Philip Brenner, "Sexuality, Political Polarization, and Survey Reports of
Religious Non-affiliation," *Politics and Religion* 12 (2019): 153.

[12]Rachel Kleinfeld, "The Rise in Political Violence in the United States

and armed demonstrations are on the increase. Organized violence is not limited to fringe and extremist groups. All of these trends put our democracy at risk by creating an intimidating environment for people, particularly women, parents, and minorities, to emerge into public service; these violent trends are also making it less safe to exercise our freedoms of speech and religion, among other things.

Beginning to Identify the Origins of the Contemporary Culture War

One way to begin identifying the origins of the contemporary culture war is by looking to the fundamentalist-modernist controversy of the early twentieth century as the flashpoint. In this book, I won't be able to develop a complete picture of the circumstances that created this controversy or the full extent of its impact on politics and the churches throughout the twentieth century. Greater detail would not help significantly advance the conversation about freedom I intend to lay out here. However, it is important to paint with a broad brush how predominantly white Christian communities had and participated in debates over the meaning of individual liberty and religious freedom in the twentieth century. With these broad strokes, we can begin to understand how these debates shape our contemporary political and religious divisions.

Beginning in the late nineteenth century and continuing through the mid-twentieth century, white mainline denominations expanded investments in liberal arts educational institutions to educate free citizens. Mainline

---

and Damage to Our Democracy," Testimony before Select Committee to Investigate the January 6th Attack on the United States Capitol, *Carnegie Endowment for International Peace* online, March 31, 2022, https://carnegieendowment.org/posts/2022/03/the-rise-in-political-violence-in-the-united-states-and-damage-to-our-democracy?lang=en.

denominations also established newspapers and journals, denominational offices, ecumenical organizations, and other institutions to provide a socially progressive and dominant voice within the public forum. For example, the Federal Council of Churches (FCC) was established in 1908 for the sake of ecumenical collaboration and became the National Council of Churches (NCC) in 1950. The FCC and NCC produced a series of social creeds that called upon the government to work toward eliminating poverty, establishing just conditions for workers and a minimum wage, legislating the regulation of the conditions of labor for women, and abolishing child labor. White mainline denominations worked in collaboration with national and global organizations such as the United Nations, and the institutions they established positioned these churches as the symbolic voice of religious pluralism, ecumenical unity, and moral authority in the United States.

In the 1920s and 1930s, white mainline Protestant denominations split over the emergence of fundamentalism and doctrinal differences. Fundamentalists believed that white mainline Protestants accommodated their faith to culture and accused them of leaning toward communism. The controversy was most intensely felt within the Northern Baptist churches and the Presbyterian Church in the USA, where fundamentalists fought to shape official doctrine and exclude modernists. Politically, white Evangelical and fundamentalist Christians advanced a grassroots movement against the teaching of evolutionary theory in public schools on the basis of a literal reading of the biblical text and in defense of their religious freedom. Baptist theologian W. T. Conner identified contrasting views of freedom within the fundamentalist and modernist movements in a 1927 article for *Social Science*. "Over against the fundamentalist insistence on authority, the modernist insists on the right of freedom of thought in religion and talks about progress in thought," Conner wrote.[13] For the fundamentalist, "the authority of the Bible (or Christ in the Bible) is an authority that liberates and sets free."[14]

Legislatures of several states introduced bills that would ban teaching evolution in public schools. The first ban bill was introduced in Kentucky in 1922 and was narrowly defeated. Opponents of the bill, such as Kentucky Rep. Bryce Cundiff, resisted because of "personal liberty."[15] Ten states, including Tennessee, introduced similar bans by 1925. The controversy culminated in the famous Scopes Monkey Trials in Dayton, Tennessee, where an adjunct science teacher was charged, tried, and found guilty of violating the Butler Act. James Reisinger, a postdoctoral research associate at the Housing Solutions Lab of New York University's Furman Center, studied the impact of the fundamentalist-modernist controversy on people in regions of the United States most affected by fundamentalism. He discovered that changes in public school teaching in these areas could be directly associated with decreases in lifetime educational attainment, "income, employment in professional occupations, and migration to cities," and an increase in inequalities.[16]

The Northern Baptist churches and Presbyterian Church in the USA ultimately defeated fundamentalism within their ranks, but the movement continued to flourish and expand into an independent network of institutions outside mainline denominations: parachurch organizations, radio stations, newspapers, and Bible colleges. Fundamentalists and Evangelicals established alternatives to progressive

---

[13]W. T. Conner, "Fundamentalism vs. Modernism," *Social Science* 2 (February, March, April, 1927): 102.

[14]Connor, "Fundamentalism vs. Modernism," 103.

[15]Keith Lawrence, "Should Leaders Follow Will of the People?" *Messenger-Inquirer*, August 3, 2014.

[16]James Reisinger, "Culture Wars and Human Capital: Evidence from the 'Fundamentalist-Modernist' Controversy," October 14, 2023, https://dx.doi.org/10.2139/ssrn.4602593.

mainline institutions and created their own newspapers and journals, such as *Christianity Today* (1956). Fuller Seminary was founded in 1947 by Charles Fuller, the host of the radio broadcast *The Old-Fashioned Revival Hour*. The school was originally intended to train young evangelists and missionaries on the West Coast. Other associations, such as the National Association of Evangelicals (1942), began around the same time.

White Protestantism as a whole became influential enough by the 1970s to be thought of as the default faith of the United States, exercising tremendous influence in shaping the nation's politics. In 1979, Jerry Falwell, pastor of Thomas Road Baptist Church and president of Liberty University, at that time known as Liberty Baptist College, founded the Moral Majority with Tim LaHaye, an American Baptist pastor and co-author of the Left Behind series, and Paul Weyrich, a conservative political activist and co-founder of the Heritage Foundation. The Moral Majority mobilized fundamentalist church leaders to emerge within the Republican political coalition and set priorities for the party platform.

In an article written for the *Fundamentalist Journal,* Falwell claimed that "liberty is the dynamic of Christianity. . . . In spite of our basic Christian love of liberty no issue has suffered more greatly throughout church history."[17] He accused the Christian left of likening liberty to "license" and those at the other end of the Christian spectrum of interpreting the meaning of freedom as "legalism." Religious liberty for fundamentalists is the freedom to preach the gospel everywhere, to educate our families, " 'train up' our children in the 'fear and admonition of the Lord,' " and "be

---

[17]Jerry Falwell, "Religious Liberty," *Fundamentalist Journal* 1, no. 2 (October 1982): 6.

forever committed to the freedom to evangelize the world."[18] Freedom from worldliness and government control created the conditions for fundamentalism to flourish.

The *Fundamentalist Journal*, in that same issue, described the centrality of the fundamentals of Christianity as the "building block in the superstructure of conservative Christianity."[19] Falwell wrote, "Whenever the judicial courts, the state and federal bureaucracies, municipal authorities, educational agencies, and social services threaten to dilute or direct the message of the Church, we must defend our basic freedom to exist in a free and pluralistic society."[20] I will develop a fuller description of the characteristics of contemporary White Christian nationalism in the first chapter. Falwell's charge to defend the basic freedom he associated with fundamentalism was central to the spiritual warfare that he envisioned would take the nation back for God.

What Exactly Is a Culture War?

A culture war is a cultural conflict between differing social groups and the struggle for dominance of their moral vision, values, beliefs, and practices.[21] Sociologist James Davidson Hunter popularized the idea in the late 1980s, when two phenomena he observed piqued his curiosity. First, he wanted to understand whether or not social, moral, and political issues that seemed on the surface to be disconnected were actually tied together in some way. For example, at that time, there were widespread demonstrations for and against banning smoking in public places, demonstrations for and against advocacy for gay rights, and

---

[18]Falwell, "Religious Liberty, 6–7."

[19]Falwell, "Religious Liberty," 7.

[20]Falwell, "Religious Liberty," 7.

[21]Philip Gorski, *American Covenant: A History of Civil Religion from the Puritans to the Present* (Princeton, NJ: Princeton University Press, 2019).

protests against the dangers posed by nuclear power. All of these movements employed similar strategies and patterns of engagement. Rather than focusing on the distinctive nature of these debates and movements, Hunter looked for connective threads. Second, he also questioned whether or not categories such as the political left and political right or those rooted in class and economic interests remained useful concepts to explain the political tensions of that time. Did they reflect the dominant axis of the political tensions?

Hunter concluded from his research that US American public culture was undergoing significant "realignment that, in turn, was generating significant tension and conflict. These antagonisms were playing out not just on the surface of social life . . . but at the deepest and most profound levels and not just at the level of ideology but in its public symbols, its myths, its discourse, and through the institutional structures that generate and sustain culture."[22] Underneath the social struggle, he found a deeper crisis over the meaning and purpose of core institutions of US society and the relationship between ideas of individual liberty and collective responsibility to each other. The conflict was primarily found between two groups: those who appealed to the traditions of the past as a guide for navigating the challenges of the present and appealed to a transcendent authority, and those who were ambivalent at best about the legacy of the past and rejected most if not all fixed standards.[23]

Hunter's observations are worth revisiting when considering the realignment of US public culture at the present moment. Differing and competing views of freedom amid the contemporary culture war reflect more than a political

---

[22]James Davison Hunter, "The Enduring Culture War," in *Is There a Culture War?: A Dialogue on Values and American Public Life*, by James Davison Hunter, Alan Wolfe, E. J. Dionne, and Michael Cromartie (Washington, DC: Brookings Institution Press, 2006).

[23]Hunter, "The Enduring Culture War."

divide. They reflect the changing religious landscape accompanied by the rise, decline, and transformation of white Christian America.

Today, twin forces of demographic change and religious disaffiliation set the nation's white churches on courses of decline, significantly affecting the number of US residents identifying as Protestant by the 1990s. According to the Pew Charitable Trust, "If trends in religious switching continue, Christians could make up less than half of the US population in a few decades."[24] The religious landscape is increasingly diverse. Among US Christians, "Racial and ethnic minorities now make up 41% of Catholics (up from 35% in 2007), 24% of evangelical Protestants (up from 19%) and 14% of mainline Protestants (up from 9%)."[25] Immigration is the leading cause of the growth of non-Christian religions, particularly "Hindus and Muslims—32% of new immigrants are estimated to be adherents of other religions (versus 6% of the US population)."[26]

Robert P. Jones, president and founder of the Public Religion and Research Institute, observes that Evangelicals and Catholics discovered powerful alliances at the end of the twentieth century and began to work together on some common causes, such as abortion, religion in the public schools, and gay rights, and have been very successful in their advocacy. The last year on record in which Protestants as a whole—not just white Christians—represented a religious majority in this nation was 2008. Since 2010, there has been no Protestant voice on the nation's highest court.

---

[24]David O'Reilly, "What Is the Future of Religion in America?" *Pew Charitable Trust* online, February 7, 2023, https://www.pewtrusts.org/en/trust/archive/winter-2023/what-is-the-future-of-religion-in-america.

[25]"America's Changing Religious Landscape," *Pew Research Center* online, May 12, 2015, https://www.pewresearch.org/religion/2015/05/12/americas-changing-religious-landscape/.

[26]"Modeling the Future of Religion in America," *Pew Research Center* online, September 13, 2022, https://www.pewresearch.org/religion/2022/09/13/modeling-the-future-of-religion-in-america/.

When FreedomWorks, a conservative policy group, founded the Tea Party in 2010 to oppose President Barack Obama's health care plan, it connected the movement to a new strain of libertarian populism. This strategy reinvigorated the culture war and revived the narrative that the United States is a White Christian nation in danger of losing its identity.

President Donald Trump continues to stoke the culture war by invoking the rhetoric of freedom to appeal to and energize his base of supporters. The White Christian nationalists who stormed the Capitol on January 6, 2021, largely shared the belief that "there has been a woeful decline in America's standing in the world because of the nation's degeneracy."[27] Sixty percent of White Christian nationalists "agree with the statement that non-Christians [if elected to public office will] create immoral policies."[28] Trump characterizes his own criminal prosecution as a witch-hunt and his conviction on thirty-four felony counts as a form of government oppression. At an election rally held in the spring of 2024, he said, "When I walk into that courtroom, I know I will have the love of 200 million Americans behind me . . . and I will be fighting for the freedom of 325 million Americans."[29] Post-conviction, he "cast himself as a martyr" and said that, if they can do this to him, "[t]hey can do this to anyone. I'm willing to do whatever I have to do to save our country and save our Constitution. I don't mind."[30] Dismantling what he calls the "deep state" was a key part of the platform in his 2024 campaign. Trump promised his supporters that he would pardon insurrectionists. On

---

[27]Pamela Cooper-White, "'God, Guns, and Guts': Christian Nationalism from a Psychoanalytic Perspective," *Religions* 14 (2023): 1.

[28]Cooper-White, "'God, Guns, and Guts,'" 2.

[29]Trump Truth Social Page, April 14, 2024.

[30]Michael Sisak, Jennifer Peltz, Eric Tucker, Michelle Price, and Jill Colvin, "Guilty: Trump Becomes First Former US President Convicted of Felony Crimes," *AP News* online, May 31, 2024, https://apnews.com/article/trump-trial-deliberations-jury-testimony-verdict-85558c6d08efb434d05b694364470aa0.

his inauguration day in 2025, Trump signed an Executive Order commuting the sentences of fourteen of his supporters serving time in federal prison and granting clemency in over 1500 cases related to the January 6, 2020, attack on the Capitol. He argues that Capitol police present at the demonstration should be the ones locked up. He refers to the insurrectionists as government "hostages." At the same time, he is curtailing the freedom of others by cracking down on immigration, suspending refugee resettlement, and issuing orders that the federal government recognize only "two sexes."[31] Trump also advocates for the elimination of gender-affirming health care and bringing back large mental health institutions to re-institutionalize people experiencing serious mental illness.[32]

Much More Than the Story of White Christian America

Jones observes that it is "no longer possible to believe that white Christian America sets the tone for the country's culture as a whole."[33] White Christian America was powerful throughout the twentieth century and greatly influenced the moral agenda of the dominant culture. However, as Jones suggests, it always operated parallel to the rich religious and cultural domain of African American Protestant churches, Brown churches, and within a richer, more diverse, and pluralistic religious landscape. There is more of the story

---

[31]Lexie Schapti and Franco Ordoñez, "Trump Signs Executive Actions on Jan. 6, TikTok, Immigration, and More," *NPR* online, January 21, 2025, https://www.npr.org/2025/01/20/g-s1-43698/trump-inauguration-execu-tive-orders-2025-day-1.

[32]Jill Colvin, "Trump's Plans If He Returns to the White House Include Deportation Raids, Tariffs and Mass Firings," *AP News* online, November 12, 2023, https://apnews.com/article/trump-policies-agenda-election-2024-second-term-d656d8f08629a8da14a65c4075545e0f.

[33]Robert P. Jones, *The End of Christian America* (New York: Simon and Schuster, 2017), 39.

to tell by highlighting the influence of historically Black churches and non-Christian faith communities, solidarity protest movements, and the activism and advocacy work of groups arising outside of white Christian America. Concepts of freedom emerge in powerful and prophetic ways from the struggles of people who were and are forced into spaces of political liminality.

In 1963, Martin Luther King Jr. captured the centrality of the value of freedom in the swell of movements for civil rights and social transformation in his famous and now iconic "I Have a Dream" speech. You will remember that King delivered the speech at the March on Washington, while standing in front of the Lincoln Memorial. A century after Lincoln signed the Emancipation Proclamation, African American descendants of enslaved people were still yearning for authentic freedom. King valued freedom as the promise of democracy and the founders' promissory note given to the nation in the Constitution and Declaration of Independence. He emphasized the importance of not overlooking "the urgency of the present moment" and urged civil rights activists to keep moving forward as there were still enslaved people. Freedom, for King, was not just a value central to American democracy; freedom was a deeply religious value and covenantal promise that gave theological justification for engaging in collective action. Freedom Schools of the civil rights movement used popular education to liberate minds and educate students for democracy. Freedom Riders boarded buses throughout the Jim Crow South to challenge segregated lunch counters and bus station waiting rooms and whites-only restrooms. Buttons bore slogans like Freedom Now, We Shall Overcome, and March for Freedom. Their stories move toward a richer, more multicultural, and religiously diverse narrative, and there are more.

Feminist political activist and legal scholar Angela Davis says that "freedom emerges from the very process of struggling and, as we attempt to achieve freedom, we discover many new dimensions of the freedom we thought we knew."[34] In the United States, our dominant understandings of freedom have always been grounded in racialized and gendered social hierarchies, which define freedom and democracy in an elitist way. Davis argues that dominant concepts of freedom and protections of individual liberty are made around the assumption that the affluent white male is and should be the freest of all. And so, the majority of people still remain in the struggle for freedom. Authentic freedom must be grounded in relationship and is an ongoing praxis, a way of living and being in the world. Davis suggests that this is "the message that now the Black Lives Matter movement is trying to impart." The Black Lives Matter movement is one of many current movements that sees and affirms the place of racialized, gendered, disabled, and othered bodies at the center of freedom movements. As Davis says, "If Black Lives Matter, then all lives matter. If Native American women's lives matter, then all lives matter."[35]

Chapter Outline

This book tracks competing visions of freedom in the United States and invites reflection on the nature of authentic Christian freedom. Within the current context of political polarization and increasing violence, I want to create space for self-reflection. I urge you to join with me, in the communities in which you are involved, in cultivating deep and courageous dialogue about the meaning of freedom across political, religious, social, economic, and class divides for the sake of the larger common good, democratic

---

[34]Angela Davis, "Freedom Is a Constant Struggle," lecture given at University of Hawai'i for the Better Tomorrow Series, YouTube (May 15, 2024), https://www.youtube.com/watch?v=pPasIZ-TAZc.

[35]Davis, "Freedom Is a Constant Struggle."

institutions, and the Body of Christ. I have four primary goals for this book:

- To track competing understandings of freedom and consider misconceptions of freedom at the heart of the contemporary culture war.
- To hold the value we place upon freedom in our society in tension with our past history of settler colonialism and slavery.
- To explore the meaning of authentic Christian freedom by lifting up the experiences of people forced into spaces of political liminality and the way they struggle for and define freedom and to examine prominent biblical stories and how they inform and define notions of Christian freedom and liberation within the larger theological tradition.
- To underscore the praxis of freedom as the means to lead us to a more just and egalitarian future.

The first chapter, "Freedom amid Political Polarization," highlights competing ideas of freedom in contemporary political and religious discourse and explores dangers posed by them. On the right, I consider the notion of "freedom from" government control by illustrating the ways White Christian nationalist groups such as Moms for Liberty amplify this stance in arguments for religious freedom and liberty and for Second Amendment gun rights. On the left, I explore the concept of "freedom to" by offering an example of the sense of freedom felt by good progressive people like me to disavow responsibility for harm. People who work in the professional-managerial sector and in white-collar jobs often pride ourselves on being aligned with organizations working to eliminate poverty, academic institutions, public radio, and reliable news media and too often maintain a comfortable distance from those who work in so-called dirty jobs. The truth is that we are all immersed in and formed by the same cultural ethos. An awareness of that formation should challenge us to develop a common understanding of freedom that leads toward justice for the common good.

The Exodus story is one of the most prominent sources for Jewish and Christian reflection on liberation and informed some of the early founding fathers' concepts of freedom and liberty for our nation. This story is often told through the lens of the conquest narrative in the Bible as a simple one about winners and losers, God taking sides with only one group of people and allying Godself with the chosen ones, with Moses leading them into the Promised Land. The second chapter, "God's Freedom to Journey with Us," identifies two contrasting interpretations of the significance of the Exodus journey, considers the reception history of the story in the United States, and explores recent research done by practical theologian Kate Common on the importance of the Highland Settlements for unpacking its meaning. If we remove lenses shaded by the conquest narrative and our long history of settler colonialism, the way God journeys with the Israelites to overcome the chaos that human beings create for ourselves is revealed as the central theme of the story. From here, we can envision a world of freedom from imperialism, colonization, conquest, violence, suffering, and marginalization. God's freedom for us and vision of the Promised Land overcome erasure and concepts of individual freedom that transcend reasonable limits and sacralize violence.

The third chapter, "Freedom to Live in Self-Giving Love for the Sake of Others" looks at one of the most well-known passages in the Christian scriptures related to freedom: Galatians 5:1, 13–15. I consider how three social mystics allowed their faith and struggle for freedom to define their understanding of its meaning. For Dietrich Bonhoeffer, Pauli Murray, and Howard Thurman, authentic Christian freedom is living in self-giving love for the sake of others, a critical and engaged stance toward life. I invite you to consider the potential for this kind of freedom to transform the social, political, and economic circumstances in which we live, enabling us to interpret Christian freedom in new and expansive ways.

As our society increasingly becomes less religious, the fourth chapter, "A Unique Challenge for Religious Leaders Today," proceeds from two questions. What is our responsibility as Christians to share liberative notions of freedom that challenge ethical neutrality, total autonomy, and independence? What can we learn from contemporary movements for social change about embodying authentic Christian freedom today? Some will be concerned that religious faith can lead only to restricting personal freedom. Challenging the cultural divide through teaching, preaching, and living out visions of the freedom to live in and embrace self-giving love for others is of vital importance in transforming our social ecology. This chapter provides examples of ways communities and congregations embody authentic freedom on the front line of today's culture war and invites you to consider how you can do so within your context.

FREEDOM AMID
POLITICAL POLARIZATION

*We tear ourselves loose from the general unrigh-
teousness and build ourselves a pleasant home
in the suburbs apart—seemingly apart! But
what has really happened? . . . Is it not our very
morality which prevents our discerning that at a
hundred other points we are . . . blind and im-
penitent toward the real deep needs of existence?*
—Karl Barth, *The Word
of God and the Word of Man*

*Jesus said to them, "Give to Caesar what belongs
to Caesar and to God what belongs to God." His
reply left them overcome with wonder.*
—Mark 12:17

Competing definitions of freedom are at the heart of the
culture war. The dominant social ecology of the United
States makes it nearly impossible to envision a concept of
freedom lived fully in relationship with others—people and
the planet Earth, our home. This chapter compares prominent and competing views of freedom that inform contemporary political and religious discourse in order to identify

the dangers that they pose and disentangle debates about freedom from our long histories of conquest, colonization, and White supremacy culture.

Among political conservatives, White Christian nationalists connect a particularly restrictive Christian identity to American public life. These groups advance a hyper-individualistic understanding of freedom. The notion of "freedom from" insists on religious freedom for conservative Christians, libertarian economic policies, and freedom from government control when it impedes or disrupts their privilege. At the same time, White Christian nationalists argue for limitations to be placed on the freedom of others—women, LGBTQIA-identified persons, immigrants, refugees, and more. White Christian nationalism is not synonymous with White Evangelicalism but cannot be understood apart from it. Fears of losing their privileged social position, political influence, and personal freedoms fuel White Christian nationalist groups, making them place a high value on freedom for a particular in-group that is white, Protestant Christian, born in the United States, and socially and fiscally conservative.

Another perspective emerging in political debates about freedom is found among White liberals and moderates, with whom I share much in common. Liberals and moderates are allies in the struggles for justice and freedom of minoritized and marginalized groups. However, they often exercise the "freedom to" avoid more challenging and self-critical moral questions and stances that should be taken regarding the value of freedom in a society whose prosperity was built upon settler colonialism and the transatlantic slave trade. The paradox of freedom and slavery is built into the identity of White Christian America, along with every other institution in our society. In this chapter, I draw on the work of scholars doing white antiracism work and seeking to dismantle the US system of mass incarceration to highlight what social ethicists Jennifer McBride and Thomas Fabisiak describe as the "moralizing discourse of meritocracy."[1] Liberals and moderates, with the best intentions to realize social transformation, often assume that "our social order is now or could one day be one in which good, innocent, and deserving people" will genuinely experience freedom. This discourse can ignore the deep-seated cultural and racialized attitudes toward those seen as deserving of merit and the tremendous influence of economic and political interests.

The Characteristics of White Christian Nationalism

Identifying the characteristics of White Christian nationalism can be challenging because there isn't a common creed, confession, or statement of belief. Rather, it is a set of complex and intersecting ideologies grounded in a particular interpretation of the Christian origins of the United States and bent toward political interests. White Christian nationalism "is a social and cultural framework which seeks to marry a heavily constrained vision of Christianity to American civic life and polity such that conservative, predominantly white Evangelicalism establishes and maintains a position of explicit privilege in American society."[2] Evangelicals are indeed more likely than religiously unaffiliated residents to agree with Christian nationalist views. However, Evangelicalism or White Evangelicalism is not entirely synonymous with White Christian nationalism.

In their book *Taking America Back for God: Christian Nationalism in the United States*, Andrew Whitehead and

---

[1]Jennifer M. McBride and Thomas Fabisiak, "Bonhoeffer's Critique of Morality: A Theological Resource for Dismantling Mass Incarceration," in *Bonhoeffer, Theology, and Political Resistance,* ed. Lori Brandt Hale and W. David Hall (Lanham, MD: Lexington Books/Fortress Press, 2020), 90.

[2]Joshua Davis, Samuel Perry, and Joshua Grubbs, "Liberty for Us, Limits for Them: Christian Nationalism and American's Views on Citizen Rights," *Sociology of Religion* 85, no. 1 (Spring 2024): 61.

Samuel Perry report conclusions they have drawn about the distinctive nature of Christian nationalism after examining data from various surveys and conducting in-depth interviews with fifty people. Whitehead and Perry use six foundational propositions to measure the level of agreement with Christian nationalist beliefs. These propositions include the belief that the United States was founded as a Christian nation by and for other Christians, and the government should make a declaration to that effect. Furthermore, the government should advocate for Christian values, resist the separation of church and state, and promote the display of religious symbols in public spaces and prayer in public schools. Finally, material prosperity in the United States is evidence of God's blessing. In turn, divine retribution should be no surprise when the nation experiences hardship or falls into a state of moral decay. They identify various responses and agreements with these propositions—Ambassadors, Accommodators, Rejectors, and Resistors. Whitehead and Perry conclude that Christian nationalism involves "symbolic boundaries that conceptually blur and conflate religious identity (Christian, preferably Protestant), with race (White), nativity (born in the United States), citizenship (American), and political ideology (socially and fiscally conservative)."[3]

While White Christian nationalism is different from Evangelicalism and White Evangelicalism, it cannot be fully understood apart from Evangelicalism. White Evangelicalism presents a coherent political, theological, and social vision that is appealing to many Christians. Central theological convictions include upholding biblical authority, confessing the centrality of Christ's substitutionary atonement, articulating one's born-again experience, sustaining a patriarchal view of the good family with a strong male head of the household, and actively working to spread the

---

[3]Andrew Whitehead and Samuel Perry, *Taking America Back for God: Christian Nationalism in the United States* (New York: Oxford University Press, 2020), x.

good news of the gospel through social reforms. These beliefs express themselves in Evangelical support for public policies such as preemptive war in Iraq, condoning the torture of political prisoners, preserving and utilizing the death penalty, advocating for police in public schools, and believing in the unrestricted right for citizens to bear arms. Whitehead and Perry found in their research

> *Christian nationalism blurs symbolic boundaries by conflating devotion to country with religious identity, race, nativity, citizenship, and political ideology.*

that "roughly half of evangelicals (by some definition) embrace Christian nationalism to some degree."[4]

White Evangelicalism promotes its own consumer culture, branded by "vast religious products" promoting Evangelical tenets of belief. According to Kristin Kobes Du Mez, professor of history at Calvin University, many white Evangelicals define their identity more by watching *Fox News* and their political party affiliation than particular theological beliefs. This popular culture extends beyond Evangelical circles and reaches into mainline denominations through social and news media outlets and the sale of Christian publications and other merchandising. Du Mez says, "At times, evangelical popular culture can subvert the authority of the evangelical elite. During the Trump campaign in 2016, many pastors were surprised to learn they wielded little influence over people in the pews."[5] When compared to other religious groups, white Evangelicals demonstrate "a preference for rejecting political compromise, for strong, solitary leadership, and for breaking the rules when necessary."[6]

---

[4]Whitehead and Perry, *Taking America Back for God*, x.
[5]Kristin Kobes Du Mez, *Jesus and John Wayne: How White Evangelicals Corrupted a Faith and Fractured a Nation* (New York: Liveright, 2020), 8.
[6]Du Mez, *Jesus and John Wayne*, 5.

Grappling with the distinctive nature of White Christian nationalism is essential to understanding the polarizing political discourse in the United States today. Whitehead and Perry insist that, in addition to exploring the connection of Christian nationalism to Evangelicalism, Christian nationalism is also a political ideology that "must be examined on its own terms."[7] Christian nationalism is often the exact opposite of a religious commitment.[8] They found that nearly half of Ambassadors for Christian nationalism do not identify themselves as white Evangelicals—"more than 15 percent are Black Protestants, Jewish, unaffiliated or of non-Christian faith."[9] US Americans who adhere to Christian nationalism put their faith in the ability to achieve a political agenda above religious teaching. As a result, Christian nationalism plays a role in how Americans evaluate constitutional rights and is a powerful predictor of voting behavior. Sociological research conducted by Joshua Davis, Samuel Perry, and Joshua Grubbs shows that White Christian nationalism "is a leading predictor that Americans prioritize gun rights, religious freedom, and states' rights but deprioritize freedom of speech, the press, right to a speedy and fair trial, and protection from unlawful searches and seizures."[10] White Christian nationalists advocate for policies that deny the entry of immigrants and refugees from predominantly Muslim countries into the United States, restrict the civil liberties of Muslims, and limit women's access to reproductive care and, more specifically, abortion. These movements stand against government-supported schools, what they call the "gay agenda," women's rights movements, and prioritize the rights of the "unborn."

It is important to clearly state that nationalism is different

---

[7]Whitehead and Perry, *Taking America Back for God*, 18.
[8]Whitehead and Perry, *Taking America Back for God*, 20.
[9]Whitehead and Perry, *Taking America Back for God*, 58.
[10]Davis, Perry, and Grubbs, "Liberty for Us, Limits for Them," 60.

from patriotism. Patriotism is a feeling of self-identification with one's country and people, love and pride for one's nation, a special concern for its well-being, and a willingness to sacrifice for the good of the whole, but not necessarily at the expense of other people and nation-states, whereas nationalism is "the identification of [a] country with a historically dominant ethnic, culture, and/or religious group and a fierce loyalty to protecting that national identity."[11] Among White Christian nationalists, freedom and liberty are more likely to be valued and favored for a particular in-group that is seeking to defend itself from

> "Nationalism is different from patriotism."

perceived cultural, religious, economic, and political threats.

Whitehead and Perry attended several church worship services in congregations identifying with Christian nationalist views and found that "not only is the 'Christian nation' narrative unquestioned, but true Christians recognize the freedom Americans have been granted through God's grace and the blood of its patriots."[12] In prayer and worship, the sacrifice of women and men in the military is often equated with Jesus's own sacrifice. Drawing upon the work of sociologist Philip Gorski, they explain, "Christian nationalism is heavily connected to the idea of blood, both as a sign of ethno-national purity (thus the connection between Christian nationalism, racism, and xenophobia . . .) but also in terms of bloody conquest and sacrifice in war."[13]

Robert Jeffress, the first prominent Evangelical to announce support for Trump's bid for the presidency in 2016, pastor of First Baptist Church of Dallas, and vocal supporter of White Christian nationalism, sponsors "Freedom Sundays" at his church. In his speech "America Is a Christian

---

[11]Whitehead and Perry, *Taking America Back for God*, 25.
[12]Whitehead and Perry, *Taking America Back for God*, 77.
[13]Whitehead and Perry, *Taking America Back for God*, 78.

Nation," Jeffress described a particular view of the nation's origins, highlighting the Christian beliefs of some of the founding fathers and a series of Supreme Court decisions. He rejected the fundamental principle of disestablishment and argued that "it is impossible for the government to be neutral toward religion. Neutrality is really hostility toward religion and especially the Christian religion."[14] Recent sociological research shows that conceptions of America's origins as a Christian nation such as this are "racially coded and grounded in White supremacy, but only for those atop the racial hierarchy."[15] Religious freedom in this context is understood as a particular Christian expression of worshipping God. Terms such as nation, history, heritage, values, and culture are freighted with Whiteness. According to Jeffress, "Any nation that chooses to publicly renounce the true God in order to embrace and elevate other gods is going to face God's judgment."[16]

Pamela Cooper-White, the Christiane Brooks Johnson Professor Emerita and Dean Emerita of Psychology and Religion at Union Theological Seminary in New York, says that good Christians become attracted to White Christian nationalism because of their belief that "there has been a woeful decline in America's standing in the world because of the nation's growing degeneracy."[17] They engage in spiritual warfare for the sake of taking the nation back for God. Ethnic and religious outsiders pose a threat to White male privilege and stability. Restoring the nation to its original

---

[14]Robert Jeffress, "America Is a Christian Nation | Faith-Week 2020," First Baptist Dallas, YouTube, 2020, https://www.youtube.com/watch?v=0MYOr90CkDU.

[15]Samuel Perry, Ryon Cobb, Andrew Whitehead, and Joshua Grubbs, "Divided by Faith (in Christian America): Christian Nationalism, Race, and Divergent Perceptions of Racial Justice," *Social Forces* (December 2, 2022): 913.

[16]Jeffress, "America Is a Christian Nation."

[17]Pamela Cooper-White, "'God, Guns, and Guts': Christian Nationalism from a Psychoanalytic Perspective," *Religions* (January 2023): 1.

Christian roots bears the potential "to lead the world into godliness."[18] They aim to stop cultural revolutions, "godless socialists" and "radical leftists," and to return control of the country to white property-owning men.

In the past, sociologists have emphasized that the vast majority of those who align with most, if not all, White Christian nationalist beliefs are uneducated working-class, low-wage, or poverty-level wage earners. However, a recent study conducted by the University of Chicago shows that it is not an accurate picture. The University of Chicago Project on Security and Threats studied the demographics of people participating in the storming of the Capitol on January 6, 2021. They discovered that "the insurrectionist movement is mainstream, not simply confined to the political fringe."[19] Insurrectionists share a deep distrust of democratic institutions and believe that they are corrupt. Employment data were available for about two-thirds of those who were arrested and charged: "More than half are business owners, including CEOs, or from white-collar occupations, including doctors, lawyers, architects, and accountants."[20]

Conservative and libertarian ideologies undergird White Christian nationalist concepts of freedom and liberty. Recent research shows that "as a person more intimately intertwines 'Christian' identity with being 'truly American,' their concept of who is deserving of protection and privileges within society becomes more constrained."[21] Only a small group of people truly belongs.

Consider how freedom figures in White Christian nationalist arguments for gun rights, parental rights to define pub-

---

[18]Cooper-White, "'God, Guns, and Guts,'" 1.

[19]Robert Pape, "The Jan. 6 Insurrectionists Aren't Who You Think They Are," *Foreign Policy* online, January 2022, https://foreignpolicy.com/2022/01/06/trump-capitol-insurrection-january-6-insurrectionists-great-replacement-white-nationalism/.

[20]Pape, "The Jan. 6 Insurrectionists Aren't Who You Think They Are."

[21]Davis, Perry, and Grubbs, "Liberty for Us, Limits for Them," 64.

lic education, and to increase border security. The concept of "freedom from" figures prominently in arguments advanced by conservative groups and extremist organizations criticizing the government for failing to embody Christian values. Freedom here is imagined as loyalty to White prosperity, one's own political party, and the Christian faith.

"The Right to Keep and Bear Arms Is Not Bestowed by Man, But Granted by God to All Americans as Our Birthright."

Wayne LaPierre, a gun rights advocate and former executive vice president and CEO of the National Rifle Association, made the above claim before the Conservative Political Action Conference in 2018, a little more than a week after a mass school shooting in Parkland, Florida, left seventeen students and staff dead. LaPierre further argued that laws fail to keep people safe, so citizens should have the right to take their safety into their own hands. "Evil walks among us and God help us if we don't protect some of our kids," he proclaimed.[22] Legislators urging for stronger gun control laws want "to eliminate second amendment and our firearms freedoms so that they can eradicate all individual freedoms. . . . Their solution is to make all of you less free."[23] He claimed that the breakdown of Christian values, not access to firearms, drives gun violence. LaPierre has since been discredited for misusing NRA funds, but his comments represent well how White Christian nationalists see gun rights as a God-given freedom, which they hold to be sacred and inalienable. White Christian nationalists believe

---

[22]Wayne LaPierre, "Remarks to the Conservative Political Action Conference," C-SPAN online, February 22, 2018, https://www.c-span.org/video/?441475-3/conservative-political-action-conference-wayne-lapierre-remarks.

[23]LaPierre, "Remarks to the Conservative Political Action Conference."

in the divine inspiration of the US Constitution. Some further suggest that a belief in a God who elevates "the gun and the right to own it" inspired the drafters of the Constitution.[24]

Du Mez says that, for over half a century, Evangelicals promoted Christian "manhood" by turning Jesus into a "badass."[25] For example, the Rev. Jimmy Meeks, a retired police officer, who served for thirty-five years in law enforcement, and a Baptist minister for over forty-seven years, offers Sheepdog Seminars. He advocates for the freedom to prepare the world to make it safe. Our "Heavenly Father is a ferocious, flaming, fiery, passionate, wild, steamy, romantic, adventurous lover." Meeks believes that a portrait of Jesus as a pacifist is not biblical. "Jesus is not Mother Teresa," Meeks says. "He was a Hell Raiser. We have feminized this man." Du Mez says, "Inspired by images of heroic manhood, evangelicals fashioned a savior who would lead them into battles of their own choosing. The new, rugged Christ transformed Christian manhood and Christianity itself."[26] Du Mez titles her book in reference to a song recorded by Gaither, Alabama, and the Oak Ridge Boys called "Jesus and John Wayne," which claims Evangelical masculinity as "somewhere between Jesus and John Wayne; a cowboy and a saint, crossing the open range. I try to be more like you, Lord, but most days, I know I ain't."

Gifts of toy guns during childhood and real firearms in the transition to adolescence represent symbolic rites of passage toward Christian masculinity for White Christian nationalists. Some Evangelical churches plan Second Amendment celebrations and Gun Sundays. In 2014, the Kentucky Baptist Convention planned Second Amendment celebra-

[24]Andrew Whitehead, Landon Schnable, and Samuel Perry, "Gun Control in the Crosshairs: Christian Nationalism and Opposition to Stricter Gun Laws," *Journal of the American Sociological Association* (July 23, 2018).

[25]Du Mez, *Jesus and John Wayne*, 295.

[26]Du Mez, *Jesus and John Wayne*, 295.

tions, where churches around the state gave away guns as door prizes to lure unchurched people into congregations across the commonwealth. One gun giveaway at Lone Oak First Baptist Church in Paducah included a steak dinner and drew nearly 1,300 people. NPR interviewed a Sunday school teacher at the church, David Keele, who said about the event that "everyone he knows has a gun. The church giveaways are a rallying point. We're doing two things here. One, we're going to talk about the Second Amendment to bear arms. But that isn't the primary thing. The primary thing is [conveying our understanding of] who Jesus is."[27] Over time, among White Christian nationalists, "Jesus had become a Warrior Leader, an Ultimate Fighter, a knight in shining armor, a William Wallace, a General Patton, a never-say-die kind of guy, a rural laborer with callouses on his hands and muscles on his frame, the sort you'd find hanGing out at the NRA convention."[28]

Parental Freedom "to Shape Our Children's Souls"

When Tina Descovich, one of the co-founders of Moms for Liberty, called into the *Rush Limbaugh Show* in January 2021, she announced their agenda to take back "parental rights" in education and advance religious freedom and freedom of speech. "There is an evil working against us on a daily basis," Descovich said.[29] Much of the moral decay she identifies in the United States can be attributed to the neglect of education by conservative Christians.

Moms for Liberty was originally founded by Tiffany

[27]Blake Farmer, "Kentucky Southern Baptists Draw Crowds with Gun Giveaway," NPR online, March 10, 2014, https://www.npr.org/2014/03/10/287311237/kentucky-southern-baptists-draw-crowds-with-gun-giveaways.

[28]Du Mez, *Jesus and John Wayne*, 295.

[29]Tina Descovich, "Moms for Liberty on the Rush Limbaugh Show," *Rush Limbaugh Show* online, January 28, 2021, https://www.youtube.com/watch?v=aEIiVHvpbx8.

Justice, Tina Descovich, and Bridget Ziegler, all of whom served as Florida school board members for some time. Moms for Liberty channels the energy they gained from arguing against school closures and mask mandates during the pandemic into advocacy for book bans, limiting the discussion of gender and sexuality in public school classrooms, and opposing Newcomer Schools for immigrants. As a result of their activism, the Florida State Board of Education now directs public schools to teach children a skewed and dangerous revisionist view of US history, emphasizing that "slaves developed skills which, in some instances, could be applied for their personal benefit."[30] Parental freedom, the "sanctity of the family," and the "sanctity of the Republic" are consistent themes that surface in comments made by parents during planned demonstrations of Moms for Liberty.[31] They see themselves as "liberating" children from what they call "woke indoctrination."[32] More than three hundred Moms for Liberty chapters have been established nationwide as of 2024 and are seeking to expand. These groups intentionally support their members in running for local school boards. The Southern Poverty Law Center classified Moms for Liberty as a right-wing extremist organization because of its anti-inclusive stance and anti-government rhetoric.[33]

Moms for Liberty call themselves "joyful warriors" as they engage in advocacy work to restore their understanding of "godliness" to our educational system. Descovich,

---

[30]Brenda Alvarez, "Florida's New History Standard: 'A Blow to Our Students and Nation,'" NEA Today online, August 3, 2023, https://www.nea.org/nea-today/all-news-articles/floridas-new-history-standard-blow-our-students-and-nation.

[31]Paige Masten, "Moms for Liberty Has Big Plans for North Carolina, Its Co-Founder Says," *Charlotte Observer* online, March 27, 2024, https://www.charlotteobserver.com/opinion/article287108320.html.

[32]"Extremist Groups: Moms for Liberty," Southern Poverty Law Center, 2024, https://www.splcenter.org/fighting-hate/extremist-files/group/moms-liberty.

[33]"Extremist Groups: Moms for Liberty."

Justice, and Ziegler first organized the group to stand
against government-imposed mask and vaccine mandates
just a few days after an American Legislative Exchange
Council (ALEC) webinar on "reclaiming education."[34] The
ALEC event included a presentation by a representative
from the Heritage Foundation who "declared that 'school
choice' would become 'very important in the next couple
of years.'"[35] Some analysts suspect that the real core of
their agenda is to undermine public education and divert
government funding toward private educational institutions.
The co-founders say that Moms for Liberty is a grassroots
movement of moms led solely by volunteers. However, progressive journalists and policymakers question this claim
because of the instant promotion of Moms for Liberty by
conservative news outlets. Conservative media, such as
Tucker Carlson Tonight and Breitbart, quickly garnered
the group a national audience.

Moms for Liberty also has deep connections to conservative Republican leaders. Christian Ziegler, former chair of
Florida's Republican Party, is Bridget Ziegler's husband. The
Zieglers frequent The Hollow, an entertainment complex
built by Victor Mellor, a construction business owner. The
Hollow brings together "Republican partisans, home-school
moms, and others who shared [Mellor's] views on Donald
Trump, gun rights, and . . . vaccine and mask mandates" to
collaborate to move the nation to the far right.[36] Their collaboration has influenced Florida politics by emboldening
conservative leaders and politicians.

[34]Paige Williams, "The Right-Wing Mothers Fuelling the School-Board
Wars," *New Yorker* online, October 31, 2022, https://www.newyorker.com/
magazine/2022/11/07/the-right-wing-mothers-fuelling-the-school-board-
wars.
[35]Williams, "The Right-Wing Mothers Fuelling the School-Board War."
[36]Tim Craig, "Waterslides and Rifles: Inside Florida's Playground for
the Far Right," *Washington Post* online, December 17, 2022, https://www.
washingtonpost.com/nation/2022/12/17/sarasota-florida-far-right/.

Florida Governor Ron DeSantis commented on his understanding of freedom amid debates about government-mandated mask and vaccine mandates in his 2022 State of the State address where he said,

> While so many around the country have consigned the people's rights to the graveyard, Florida has stood as *freedom's* vanguard. . . . Florida has become the escape hatch for those chafing under authoritarian, arbitrary, and seemingly never-ending mandates and restrictions. . . . We reject the biomedical security state that curtails liberty, ruins livelihoods, and divides society. And we will protect the rights of individuals to live their lives *free* from the yoke of restrictions and mandates. . . . Florida has stood strong as the rock of *freedom*. And upon this rock, we must build Florida's future.[37]

Moms for Liberty worked closely with DeSantis on the "Parental Rights in Education" bill, which opponents call his "Don't Say Gay" legislation. The bill was signed into law in March 2022 and prohibits discussion of sexual orientation or gender identity in certain grade levels.

Joyful Warriors, a podcast sponsored by Moms for Liberty, produced an episode titled "How Do We Protect Our Given Rights?" during which Justice talks with Kristin Waggoner, president, CEO, and general counsel for the Alliance Defending Freedom. Waggoner files cases regarding religious freedom and parental rights in the courts to defend "encroachments by the government on our freedoms and liberty."[38] She says parents have the authority, privilege, and

---

[37]Ron DeSantis, "State of the State Address," 2022, https://www.flgov.com/2022/01/11/governor-ron-desantis-state-of-the-state-address-3/.

[38]"How Do We Protect Our Given Rights?" *Joyful Warriors Podcast,* December 4, 2023, https://open.spotify.com/episode/4oGWRdIvx9mn4z SQ87hPBM.

freedom "to shape our children's souls" and has worked closely with Moms for Liberty to craft the "Promise to America's Parents." Waggoner is an originalist, believing that the Constitution should only be understood in ways consistent with the founding fathers' original intent.

Moms for Liberty enlists the support of Black conservatives for the sake of its cause, but the way in which the group conveys its ideas of freedom, the identity of our nation, its understanding of US culture, and its retelling of our nation's history upholds systems and structures of White supremacy. For example, at a school board meeting in Williamson County, Tennessee, a local Moms for Liberty group staged a demonstration as the superintendent's contract was under review. One white demonstrator said, "We're gonna replace every board member here with people *just like me*. Nothing would make us happier than to surround you with a roomful of Americans who believe in the Constitution of the United States and Jesus Christ above!"[39]

"The Bible says even Heaven is going to have a wall around it."

Seldom is the term "freedom" used in public debates about immigration policy, but understanding the value and concept of freedom is about much more than grappling with specific uses of the term. Immigration restrictions have always been about much more than movement across borders of nation-states. Jay Dolmage, associate professor of English at the University of Waterloo and a scholar of disability studies, observes that the enactment of restrictive immigration policies since the 1920s has always been about maintaining the social power of certain groups—white, wealthy, able-bodied, and Christian—and a very public pro-

---

[39]Williams, "The Right-Wing Mothers Fueling the School-Board War."

cess of the stigmatization of other people's bodies, beliefs, and behaviors and the limitation of their freedom.

Referring to the work of political scientist Aristide Zolberg, Dolmage writes, "American immigration policy has always had a double logic: 'boldly inclusive' and 'brutally exclusive.' "[40] The Statue of Liberty symbolizes the "freedom of humanity" as she has stood in New York harbor since 1886, adorned with a plaque displaying the famous words of Emma Lazarus's poem "The New Colossus."

> "Give me your tired, your poor,
> Your huddled masses yearning to breathe free,
> The wretched refuse of your teeming shore.
> *Send these, the homeless, tempest-tossed to me,*
> *I lift my lamp beside the golden door!"*

Contrary to the storied welcoming gaze of the Statue of Liberty, Ellis Island was a "key laboratory and theater for eugenics."[41] Ellis Island employed the power of the assembly line to classify migrants according to race, ethnicity, nationality, and physical ability. For Dolmage, the mechanization and power of the assembly represented more than the efficiency of a plant, it expressed a broader "cultural logic" through which the bodies of people seen as inferior and defective could be refused and rejected.

Today, the ideology and advocacy of White Christian nationalism is increasingly visible and influential in public debates over immigration policy. Studies show that "Christian nationalism is a robust determinant of immigrant animus."[42] Support for restrictive immigration policies is

---

[40]Jay Dolmage, *Disabled upon Arrival: Eugenics, Immigration, and the Construction of Race and Disability* (Columbus: Ohio State University Press, 2018), Kindle edition.

[41]Dolmage, *Disabled upon Arrival.*

[42]As cited by Laura Alexander, "Proposition 187 and the Travel Ban: Addressing Economy, Security, and White Christian Nationalism in US Chris-

usually expressed in terms of border control and security, but much more is happening here. Immigration is a symbol that "America's religious and cultural landscape is being fundamentally altered," and the influx of immigrants from predominantly Muslim countries and Latin America threatens the narrative of the identity of the United States as a Christian nation.[43]

Attitudes about undocumented immigration held by White Christian nationalists reflect concerns about their own economic freedom and prosperity, the ability of immigrants to assimilate into a perceived dominant and normative White Christian culture, and prejudice against people who are Muslim and Latinx. Additionally, descriptors such as Muslim and Latinx are also understood as racial categories and identified with Black and Brown within the dominant culture.[44]

Although it was written before the Trump presidency, a chorus from the Broadway musical *Hadestown* evidences these beliefs.

> Why do we build the wall?
> We build the wall to keep us free . . .
> How does the wall keep us free?
> The wall keeps out the enemy . . .
> Who do we call the enemy?
> The enemy is poverty
> And the wall keeps out the enemy
> And we build the wall to keep us free
> That's why we build the wall
> We build the wall to keep us free.[45]

---

tian Communities," *Religions* 13 (January 1, 2022): 4.

[43]Robert P. Jones, *The End of White Christian America* (New York: Simon and Schuster, 2016), 42.

[44]See Alexander, "Proposition 187 and the Travel Ban."

[45]Anaïs Mitchell, "Why We Build the Wall," *Hadestown: Original*

Among those who agree with White Christian nationalism, over half believe that non-Christians will create "immoral policies." In 2018, Robert Jeffress was interviewed by
Fox News regarding Trump's series of Executive Orders to
prevent Muslims from certain countries entering the United
States. Jeffress assured Trump that "Jesus was saying God
has given government unique authority and responsibility
and that chief responsibility is to protect citizens from evil
doers." At Trump's inauguration, Jeffress chose to preach
about God telling Nehemiah to build a wall around Jerusalem. "God is not against walls. Walls are not unchristian.
The Bible says even heaven is going to have a wall around
it. Not everyone is going to be let in."[46]

President Donald Trump continued to appeal to White
Christian nationalist beliefs as he campaigned for reelection. In a speech given in Iowa in December 2023, he stood
between two Christmas trees and claimed that immigrants
from Africa, Asia, and South America were "destroying
the blood of our country" and "going after Christians in
America." Additionally, he defended Christianity in America
and vowed to "create a federal task force on fighting anti-
Christian bias to investigate any 'discrimination, harassment
and persecution.' "[47]

Freedom among White Allies for Racial Justice

The title of this chapter, "Freedom amid Political Polarization," implies that differing concepts of freedom exist

---

Broadway Cast Recording (2019), https://www.youtube.com/watch?v=
GbkurQ00-EU.

[46]"Pastor Robert Jeffress on Border Security," *Fox News* online, December 22, 2018, https://www.facebook.com/watch/?v=2636636066361449.

[47]Michael Gold, "Trump, Attacked for Echoing Hitler, Says He Never
Read 'Mein Kampf,' " *New York Times* online, December 19, 2023, https://
www.nytimes.com/2023/12/19/us/politics/trump-immigrants-hitler-mein-
kampf.html.

in tension with one another in our society. Thus far, I have only explored ideals of freedom being advanced by conservatives and White Christian nationalist groups. In this section, I explore additional concepts of freedom emerging among many white liberals and moderates who identify as mainline Protestants and with whom I share a great deal in common. These groups identify as allies of the work of racial justice and, at the same time, often fail to acknowledge the racism inherent within their concepts of freedom. Modern and Western ideals of separative individualism, autonomy, and the sovereignty of the white subject undergird dominant concepts of freedom in mainline Protestant denominations.

In this section, I focus on three examples: the belief that people with social privilege can somehow distance themselves from others due to wealth or a sense of moral righteousness, the tragic irony of holding freedom in such high regard in a carceral state, and liberties taken by white allies in the struggle for civil rights and racial justice to avoid full complicity in practices of harm. Remember that one of the goals for this book is to track competing understandings of freedom and situate these values within their differing contexts in order to expose dangers that they present and to nurture the art of talking across lines of social, economic, and political difference. In these few pages, I intend to examine my own personal relationship to these debates as a scholar, professor, and white religious leader in a predominantly white mainline denomination.

Imagining There Are People with Whom One Shares Nothing in Common

Thomas Fabisiak has taught non-credit classes in theology and ethics at Arrendale State Prison since 2012 and currently serves at the director of the Chillon Project at Life University. The Chillon Project offers courses and degree programs to people in prison and the formerly incarcerated in the state of Georgia. Their programs cultivate learning communities grounded in principles and practices of compassion and conflict resolution. Jennifer McBride, associate rector of formation at All Saints' Episcopal Church in Atlanta, Georgia, works with members of her congregation on the "Freedom Writers" project, a letter-writing project that serves as a form of visitation with incarcerated people. McBride and Fabisiak draw on the writings of theologian Dietrich Bonhoeffer to interrogate the prevalent assumption in our society that people with social and economic freedom can distance themselves from others as if they share nothing in common with them. Through their work, they examine the moral foundation upon which the prison system is built.

I will go into greater detail about Bonhoeffer's understanding of Christian freedom in chapter 4, but I want to discuss here how he challenged the idea that "Christian faithfulness may be expressed through human standards of morality."[48] Like the Reformed theologian Karl Barth, Bonhoeffer suggests that socially and economically privileged Christians can never "exonerate themselves from present complicity in social sin and injustice."[49] Barth calls this "bourgeois morality" through which "privileged Christians not only blind themselves to the ways their lives effortlessly benefit from and uphold an unjust status quo, they also distance themselves from other human beings who suffer societal harm."[50] Both Barth and Bonhoeffer recognized that, within their context, it was easy to convict people who orchestrated violence and committed evil acts, such as executioners, members of the Gestapo, or those who first envisioned the Final Solution. But in reality the moral

---

[48]McBride and Fabisiak, "Bonhoeffer's Critique of Morality," 92.
[49]McBride and Fabisiak, "Bonhoeffer's Critique of Morality," 92.
[50]McBride and Fabisiak, "Bonhoeffer's Critique of Morality," 92.

formation of both sinners and those who see themselves as morally righteous occurs within the same social ethos. God alone is righteous, and righteousness cannot be encapsulated in a particular sense of moral duty or understood apart from Jesus's way of being in the world.

Conservative and White Christian nationalist groups articulate a clear boundary between who is righteous and unrighteous, deserving and undeserving of freedom as illustrated in previous examples in this chapter. There are also many indirect ways that social groups communicate their understanding of the difference between deserving and undeserving people in a society. For example, social and economic privilege allows "good people" to maintain distance from other social groups. Liberals, moderates, and Progressives can practice a politics of alignment in their own ways by reinforcing and affirming the goodness of people who listen to public radio, read the *New York Times* and the *Atlantic*, and graduate from prestigious institutions.

Growing up in a liberal Southern Baptist household often under fire during the culture war of the 1980s and 1990s, this politics of alignment was certainly an aspect of my own experience and formation. My father often wore a red "Fundamentalist Anonymous" baseball cap. The trauma my parents and family experienced as a result of institutional changes imposed by fundamentalists within the Southern Convention and at Southern Baptist Theological Seminary reinforced a strong commitment to liberal theology. Compromise could lead to stepping into a moral rut. I have often taken similar positions, but I wonder, after reading McBride's and Fabisiak's research, if offloading the responsibility to be in conversation with people holding radi-

> *Social groups communicate their understanding of the difference between deserving and undeserving in many indirect ways.*

cally different views of religious freedom and individual liberty prevents the capacity to build broader networks of social solidarity and intracommunal understandings of freedom. More alarmingly, Fabisiak and McBride suggest that practicing a politics of alignment can reassert a core ideology upon which the carceral state depends—the idea that there are people who belong in the categories of being deserving and undeserving. What is the most effective way to relate to people who are "outside" of my political or social alignments in order to build broader networks of social solidarity and intracommunal understandings of freedom? This is the question with which I must continue to grapple.

The Tragic Irony of Holding Freedom as a Cherished Value in a Carceral State

According to the most recent studies, "the United States has experienced a 500 percent increase in rates of incarceration over the last forty years."[51] That means that 2.3 million people are in prison or jail. Thus, one out of every thirty-one US Americans is in prison, jail, or on probation. One in three men identified as African American and one in six Latino or Hispanic men can expect to be incarcerated at some point in their lives; that is compared to one of out every seventeen white men.[52] People of Color make up about 30 percent of the US population and 60 percent of the prison population. Fabisiak and McBride observe that mass incarceration "carries on elements of slavery, Jim Crow, settler colonialism, and racial terror by other means, and that it produces and depends upon racialized ideas of 'criminality.' "[53] The system depends upon the racialized

---

[51]McBride and Fabisiak, "Bonhoeffer's Critique of Morality," 89.

[52]"Mass Incarceration: An Animated Series," American Civil Liberties Union online, 2024.

[53]McBride and Fabisiak, "Bonhoeffer's Critique of Morality," 90.

theories of people who are deserving and undeserving that are part of our dominant culture.

Additionally, segregation is alive and well across America's landscape. The Brookings Institution reports:

> The neighborhood of an average white resident in the 100 largest metropolitan areas became slightly less white between 2000 and 2018, decreasing from 79 percent white to 71 percent. More notably during this period, the neighborhood of the average Black resident crossed the threshold from majority-Black to a diverse plurality because of Latino or Hispanic population growth.[54]

Policing responds to segregated landscapes, constructing and maintaining them. Daanika Gordon, associate professor of sociology at Tufts University, rode along with police officers in two different districts in a Rust Belt city to compare policing in predominantly white and Black neighborhoods. Her study found "officers navigating two worlds: one characterized by punitive social control, a sense of relentless work, and antagonistic attitudes toward the public; the other by responsive police service, ample resources for preventative work, and a sense of citizens' worthiness."[55] The predominantly Black neighborhood was overpoliced for surveillance and social control and underpoliced for emergency services. In predominantly white neighborhoods,

[54]Christopher Coes, Jennifer S. Vey, and Tracy Hadden Loh, "The Great Real Estate Reset: Separate and Unequal—Persistent Residential Segregation Sustaining Racial and Economic Injustice in the US," *The Brookings Institution* online, December 16, 2020, https://www.brookings.edu/articles/the-great-real-estate-reset-a-data-driven-initiative-to-remake-how-and-what-we-build/.

[55]Daanika Gordon, *Policing the Racial Divide: Urban Growth Politics and the Remaking of Segregation* (New York: New York University Press, 2022), 6.

the police reproduced historic patterns of institutional investment and protection.

McBride and Fabisiak assert that systems and structures of a society that orchestrates such widespread racialized violence train people to go against their natural intuitions. In truth, it is not so easy and straightforward to parse out the deserving from the undeserving in our culture. Many of the people who get trapped within the system of mass incarceration have been treated violently themselves. One recent study conducted of people who have been released from prison within the last year found that 40 percent witnessed someone being killed, 50 percent had been beaten by their parents, and 16 percent experienced sexual abuse.[56] There really are no innocent bystanders, even among those who believe they can distance themselves financially, vocationally, or physically from the criminal justice system or other forms of violence.

White Allies with the Freedom to Avoid Claiming Full Complicity with Practices and Policies Causing Harm

Jennifer Harvey, vice president for academic affairs and academic dean at Garrett Evangelical Theological Seminary, writes extensively about racial justice and work to be done regarding white antiracism. She includes a chapter on the mainline Protestant denominations' reception of "The Black Manifesto" in her book *Dear White Christians: For Those Still Longing for Racial Reconciliation.* James Forman interrupted Sunday worship at Riverside Church in New York City on May 4, 1969, and called upon white churches and Jewish synagogues to pay Black people of the country $500 million in reparations for Black enslavement—"fifteen dollars for every Black brother and sister in the United States."

---

[56]McBride and Fabisiak, "Bonhoeffer's Critique of Morality," 97.

"The Black Manifesto" had a troubled reception from its first day. White Evangelical churches immediately expressed outrage. *Christianity Today* published an editorial casting Forman "as a key formulator of the new anti-church revolution."[57] The National Black Economic Development Conference endorsed the manifesto, and it was presented to a wide variety of ecclesial bodies, including the National Council of Churches, Episcopal Church, United Methodist Church, and Lutheran Church of America, among others. The mainline denominations took stands as allies of the civil rights movement, and many endorsed reparations, but as they debated reparations and established funds for programming, they failed to accept the demands of Black clergy, often appointed their own leadership to committees to determine how funds would be used, and did not channel money to Black-led organizations. Harvey says that the failure of white denominations to remember this history should affect our understanding of white Christian involvement in struggles for racial justice, civil rights, and freedom. Furthermore, this failure continues to influence "our relationships with Black Christians that remain deeply unresolved, despite the four decades that have since passed."[58]

In his 1963 essay titled "Letters to a White Liberal," the Trappist monk Thomas Merton described the struggle for freedom during the civil rights movement as much more than a struggle for equality, rights, and freedom for African Americans. For Merton, the civil rights movement was a struggle to experience true freedom within the heart of whites. He charged the dominant Southern white society with promoting a delusional idea of freedom for whites

---

[57]Jennifer Harvey, *Dear White Christians: For Those Still Longing for Racial Reconciliation* (Grand Rapids, MI: William B. Eerdmans, 2014), 120.

[58]Harvey, *Dear White Christians*, 127.

while denying freedom for Black and Brown people and enforcing segregation and the rule of law through violent means. He wrote, "Societies which 'experience their reality' on [an] oniric and psychopathic level are precisely those whose members are most convinced of their own rightness, their own integrity, indeed their own complete moral infallibility."[59] Merton observed that the white experience of unreality was the flashpoint of racial conflict. Many liberal and progressive Protestants and Catholics at the time remained "at best confused and evasive in their sympathies" with the struggle for civil rights for African Americans. Even liberal and progressive white Christians held onto an "implicit and axiomatic assumption of white superiority" and the presumed freedom to avoid full complicity with practices and policies causing harm.[60]

Reparations are about freedom, freedom from bondage and oppression, and repairing the harm done by our long history of settler colonialism, colonization, and conquest. This history has led to long-standing racialized disparities in income and wealth, health outcomes, incarceration rates, educational attainment, and overall quality of life. The practice of repairing harm "assumes and acknowledges relationship and a shared history."[61]

Closing Thoughts

The perspectives explored here constrain a more authentic, expansive, and theologically rich social and moral imagination for freedom. At the present moment, polarization plays more of a defining factor for informing prominent

---

[59]Thomas Merton, "Letters to a White Liberal," *Blackfriars* 44, no. 521 (November 1963): 506.

[60]Merton, "Letters to a White Liberal," 509–10.

[61]Harvey, *Dear White Christians*, 129.

views of freedom than commitments to justice, social solidarity, and the common good. From a Christian theological
perspective, polarization plays more of a defining factor
for freedom than the distinctive way of following Jesus in
the world. As Martin Luther King Jr. famously proclaimed,
"There is no freedom until we all are free." Political philosophers such as John Rawls argue that self-respect, mutual respect, and social cooperation are the preconditions of freedom and are foundational to establishing authentic communities of belonging.

> "From a Christian theological perspective, polarization plays more of a defining factor for freedom than the distinctive way of following Jesus in the world."

Contemporary debates about religious freedom and
individual liberties suggest that we need a thicker description of freedom that is rooted in the understanding that we
exist in relationship, and that our actions affect others, and
that transcends religious and political affiliations to inform
a more collaborative political vision for our democracy.
Religious traditions have much to offer when cultivating a
theologically rich understanding of authentic freedom. As
a Christian theologian, I focus on freedom defined by my
own tradition but also consider those teachings within the
religiously diverse landscape of the ancient and contemporary worlds. Defining authentic freedom must also be
an intracommunal task. Authentic freedom emerges in the
struggle against oppression and as one actualizes the fullness of self in community.

2

GOD'S FREEDOM
TO JOURNEY WITH US

The Empire, leaving nothing in its wake un-
touched, has died, it is dying, it will die. In its
time, Empire was known by many names and
personas across many cultures and lands. Among
the most well-known of those names has been
militarism, greed, white supremacy, capitalism,
and colonialism.

—Chase Tibbs and Greg Jarrell
"Obituary for the Empire"

Then Moses stretched out his hand over the sea.
The Lord pushed the sea back by a strong east
wind all night, turning the sea into dry land. The
waters were split into two. The Israelites walked
into the sea on dry ground. The waters formed
a wall for them on their right hand and on their
left. The Egyptians chased them and went into the
sea after them, all of Pharaoh's horses, chariots,
and cavalry. As morning approached, the Lord
looked down on the Egyptian camp from the
column of lightning and cloud and threw the
Egyptian camp into a panic. The Lord jammed

> *their chariot wheels so that they wouldn't turn*
> *easily. The Egyptians said, "Let's get away from*
> *the Israelites, because the Lord is fighting for*
> *them against Egypt!" Then the Lord said to Mo-*
> *ses, "Stretch out your hand over the sea so that the*
> *water comes back and covers the Egyptians, their*
> *chariots, and their cavalry." So Moses stretched*
> *out his hand over the sea. At daybreak, the sea*
> *returned to its normal depth. The Egyptians*
> *were driving toward it, and the Lord tossed the*
> *Egyptians into the sea. . . . The Israelites, however,*
> *walked on dry ground through the sea. The waters*
> *formed a wall for them on their right hand and*
> *on their left.*
>
> —Exodus 14:21–27, 29

Some people will question whether or not belief in God and human freedom are truly compatible ideas. Historically, that was one of the big questions that came out of the European Enlightenment of the eighteenth century. For me, authentic freedom is grounded in the belief in a God who accompanies people and the planet in the struggle for freedom. Authentic freedom claims life in the face of death-dealing oppressive regimes. The journey of the Israelites' departure from Egypt, crossing the Red Sea, is one of the most influential and frequently referenced biblical stories for shaping Jewish and Christian notions of freedom and liberation.

It can be told as a simple story about winners and losers. God takes sides with one group of people and allies Godself with the chosen ones as Moses leads them into the Promised Land. But there is an oppressive side to the way we remember and interpret the Exodus journey in US culture. Particularly among white Christians and in our churches, this story has been interpreted as God offering the promise of a new life and new land only to a chosen few, justifying the conquest of others in the name of that promise.

As we return to the biblical narrative in our contemporary era and consider more authentic notions of Christian freedom and religious liberty, it is critical to remember that sacred texts and stories were produced through complex processes in the shadow of ancient empires. Moreover, we are now reading these stories in contexts shaped by modern colonization. Postcolonial theorist Hulisani Ramantswana uses the concept of "double consciousness" to unpack the pluri-voiced nature of biblical stories.[1] First articulated by the sociologist and pan-Africanist W. E. B. Du Bois in essays included in *The Souls of Black Folk*, "double consciousness" highlights the struggle for social identity, which he describes as "a peculiar sensation . . . the sense of always looking at oneself through the eyes of others, of measuring one's soul by the tape of a world that looks on in amused contempt and pity."[2]

You may wonder how someone occupying my own social location—a white feminist theological ethicist from the United States, firmly situated in the middle class—identifies with postcolonial readings of the Bible. What I am trying to get into here is the experiential world and theological imagination of the people whose stories are told in the Bible. The Bible is a library of the stories of ancient migrants. Investigating the many voices and circumstances remembered in biblical stories invites me to unpack a deeper meaning of these stories that describe a very different social location than my own and to cultivate awareness of the distinctive way the experience of heading out into the wilderness to flee persecution forms people. Reading from different perspectives and listening to multiple voices increases my understanding of how interpreting the Bible from a posi-

---

[1] Hulisani Ramantswana, "Sacred Texts Produced under the Shadow of Empires: Double Consciousness and Decolonial Options in Reading the Bible," *Old Testament Essays* 36, no. 1 (2023): 236.

[2] W. E. B. Du Bois, "Of Our Spiritual Strivings," in *The Souls of Black Folk* (Project Gutenburg eBook #408, 2021).

tion of social privilege can be used to justify oppression, violence, and colonization. Alternatively, challenging myself to put on the lenses of different experiences gives insight into ways people living in vulnerable situations overcome social hierarchies, create communities of solidarity, surpass the myth of redemptive violence, and embody freedom.

In this chapter, I invite you to consider the social and political influence of the Exodus story in the US context and then to remove lenses shaded by our long history of settler colonialism, investigating the meaning of the story in fresh, new ways. Several questions guide my inquiry: How do we challenge notions of freedom and liberation that preserve remnants of colonial functioning in US society? Can we articulate and value liberation and freedom in ways that embrace a vision of the Promised Land that no longer connects the theological idea of chosenness to specific nation-states or perpetuates patriarchy, racial hierarchies, slavery, colonization, oppression, and violence? How can interpretations of the Exodus story call for the liberation of the oppressed while, at the same time, consider the possibility that those who God liberates always risk becoming oppressors themselves? Research done by American religious historians and biblical scholars along with arguments made by postcolonial, Black, feminist, womanist, and queer theologians are particularly helpful in my search to answer these questions. These scholars disconnect the conquest narrative in the Bible from the story of the Israelites' escape from Egypt.

> *"Challenging myself to put on the lenses of different experiences gives insight into ways people living in vulnerable situations overcome social hierarchies, create communities of solidarity, surpass the myth of redemptive violence, and embody freedom."*

Authentic freedom is encountered in the people's response to their wilderness experience. Rather than continuing to perpetuate the idea that freedom can be secured by military might, liberation becomes known in the transformation of death-dealing systems and structures that were created by oppressive regimes and the formation of communities of solidarity. Freedom is not an exclusive territory defined by the boundaries of particular nation-states, geographical regions, or even a single religious identity. Authentic freedom is a state of being in the world, a critical and engaged stance that claims peace in the face of physical threats, life over against structures intended to ensure social death, and hope embodied in community.

The Social and Political Influence of the Exodus Narrative in the US Context

Biblical scholars interpreting ancient stories do much more than research their meaning within their original context. They also explore how communities receive these stories over time and their social and political influence. Since the colonial era, US Americans have returned to the Exodus story as a paradigm for liberation and freedom. Our nation's long history of colonization and conquest figures prominently in the ways US Americans articulate the meaning of the Exodus journey.

Some, in positions of power, have read the narrative in light of their claim to the divine right to settle and colonize the land or later through the perspective of living in well-established communities and churches. The Exodus story has

> *"Our nation's long history of colonization and conquest figures prominently in the ways US Americans articulate the meaning of the Exodus journey."*

been used as a theological ground to validate political dominance and establish or perpetuate White supremacist systems and structures. Others, including enslaved people, abolitionists, and civil rights activists, drew on the Exodus story to claim God's liberation of people from bondage and to emphasize how God sides with the oppressed. In contrast to these two perspectives, Indigenous people identify more with the Canaanites as the original inhabitants of the Promised Land and emphasize that the God who delivers and liberates is known by others as One who conquers.

Examples of Exoduses in America

The Exodus story loomed large in the writings of Protestant magisterial reformers and greatly influenced Puritan and Pilgrim self-understanding as a chosen people as they crossed the Atlantic Ocean, headed to settle and colonize the North American continent. Steadfast to the reformers' commitment to interpreting their experiences in light of the biblical narrative, Puritans saw themselves on an exodus journey, fleeing the oppression of the Roman Catholic Church, its alliances with monarchies across Europe, and the Anglican theocracy of England.

Many Puritan sermons compared North America to Canaan and the Promised Land and compared Native Americans to Hivites, Canaanites, and Hittites. John Cotton, the leading minister of the Massachusetts Bay Colony, proclaimed, "This placing of people in this or that Countrey, is from God's Soveraignty over all the Earth, and the Inhabitants thereof: as in *Psal.* 24. 1. *The Earth is the Lords, and the fulness thereof.* And in *Jer.* 10. 7. God is there called, *The King of Nations?* . . . God's people take the Land by *Promise:* and therefore the Land of *Canaan* is called a Land of Promise."[3]

---

[3] "God's promise to his plantations; [Three lines from Samuel] / As it was

Not all colonists shared the belief that God gave them the right to colonize the Atlantic coast of North America as a Promised Land. Anglicans in Virginia and leaders of other colonies, such as the Baptist Roger Williams, envisioned a more expansive understanding of divine providence and religious freedom. For example, Williams challenged the fusion of religious and political authority in the Massachusetts Bay Colony and was exiled over disagreements with Puritan governance. He argued that forced worship led to religious warfare and advocated that colonists purchase Native American land. Williams appealed to the book of Ezra as the grounds of religious liberty because the Persian King Artaxerxes supported the Jewish people. He founded the city of Providence and established the colony of Rhode Island, which became a haven for people persecuted for their religious beliefs, including Native Americans, Quakers, and Jews.

Some of the founding fathers of the nation believed that the imagery of the Israelites crossing the Red Sea held great potential to rally colonists to revolt against Great Britain. Just a few months after colonists in North America declared independence from British colonial rule, a small committee was formed to design the nation's seal. Benjamin Franklin, Thomas Jefferson, and John Adams conceived of their own designs and ultimately proposed to the Continental Congress that the Great Seal of the United States depict Moses and the Israelites standing on the shore of the Promised Land, watching as the waters of the Red Sea drown the Egyptians. The motto encircling the seal read "Rebellion to Tyrants and Obedience to God." While the Continental Congress rejected their proposal, it shows the appeal of the image to some colonists as divine inspiration for violent revolution and

---

delivered in a sermon by John Cotton, B.D. and preacher of God's word in Boston. [Seven lines from Psalms]." In the digital collection *Evans Early American Imprint Collection* (University of Michigan Library Digital Collections, 2024), https://quod.lib.umich.edu/e/evans/.

casts revolt against England as an act of obedience to God.

These observations should not suggest that the founding fathers embraced an understanding of individual liberty established for all. In 1775, when a warship first unfurled the flag with the battle cry "Don't Tread on Me" to declare independence from British rule, freedom was both a highly valued and contested idea. The majority of settler-colonists and the founding fathers of our nation were shaped by a Western Christian theological imagination, which informed their understanding of social hierarchies, including the Doctrine of Discovery. While a portion of tolerance of diverse religious beliefs could be found in some colonies, the birth of White freedom for settler-colonists forged a path of destruction of the life, lands, and spiritual homes of Indigenous peoples, and the founding fathers held close to "the bosom of a slave society."[4] Thomas Jefferson, widely remembered as the father of our democracy, believed in the natural and social inferiority of enslaved people and argued that they should be colonized elsewhere. Jefferson wrote,

> When we compare [freed black slaves] with the writers of the race among whom he lived, and particularly with the epistolary class, in which he has taken his own stand, we are compelled to enroll him at the bottom of the column. . . . The improvement of blacks in body and mind, in the first instance of their mixture with whites, has been observed by everyone, and proves that their inferiority is not the effect merely of their condition of life.[5]

---

[4]Barbara Chase-Riboud, "Slavery and Public History: An International Symposium," a paper given for the Eighth Annual Gilder Lehrman Center International Conference, Yale University, New Haven, CT, November 2–4, 2006.

[5]As quoted by Keeanga-Yamahtta Taylor, *From #BlackLivesMatter to Black Liberation* (Chicago: Haymarket Books, 2014), 23.

Deliverance of the colonists from religious and political oppression in Europe did not equate with the establishment of a land of freedom for all.

The understanding of freedom and liberation that emerges out of the context of settler-colonialism has always been incomplete. Historian Roxanne Dunbar-Ortiz says that "'free' land was the magnet that attracted European settlers. Many were slave owners who desired limitless land for lucrative cash crops."[6] From the very beginning, "the form of colonialism that the Indigenous peoples of North America have experienced was modern . . . the expansion of European corporations, backed by government armies, into foreign areas, with subsequent expropriation of lands and resources. Settler colonialism is a genocidal policy."[7] As a member and citizen of the Osage Nation, Robert Allen Warrior, the Hall Distinguished Professor of American Literature and Culture at the University of Kansas, reads the story of Exodus through the experience of the Canaanites. The native people of Canaan are displaced from their land and only have status if they honor the covenant offered to the Israelites. He writes, "A delivered people is not a free people, nor is it a free nation. People who have survived the nightmare of subjugation dream of escape."[8] God goes before the Israelites to "defeat the indigenous inhabitants of Canaan."[9] But the God who delivers also conquers.

> And I have promised to bring you up out of your misery in Egypt into the land of the Canaanites, Hittites,

---

[6] Roxanne Dunbar-Ortiz, *An Indigenous Peoples' History of the United States* (Boston: Beacon Press, 2015), 3.

[7] Dunbar-Ortiz, *An Indigenous Peoples' History*, 6.

[8] Robert Allen Warrior, "Canaanites, Cowboys, and Indians: Deliverance, Conquest, and Liberation Theology Today," *Christianity and Crisis* 49 (September 11, 1989): 262.

[9] Warrior, "Canaanites, Cowboys, and Indians," 262.

Amorites, Perizzites, Hivites and Jebusites—a land
flowing with milk and honey. (Exodus 3:17)

Warrior argues that there is a "two-ness" to the way the
ancient Israelites' self-definition of freedom and liberation
is described—at the same time anti-hierarchic and anti-
imperial yet also a covenant for chosen people that can
reflect the imperial mind-set and identity.

Enslaved peoples in the United States held onto the
deepest conviction that their oppressors were the pharaohs
of this land. Preachers in the diaspora proclaimed God's
deliverance from their white oppressors before, during,
and after the revolution. Alphonso Saville, assistant professor of American religious history at Union Presbyterian
Seminary, studies the diverse religious cultures contributing
to the formation of African American Christianity in the
seventeenth century. The experiences of John Marrant, the
first ordained Black pastor in North America, are recorded
in *A Narrative of the Lord's Wonderful Dealings with John
Marrant: A Black, Born in New York in North America.*
In his narrative, Marrant conjured "the Exodus story to
denounce American slavery. His employment of that story
utilizes symbols—blood and wilderness—to depict a narrative of retaliation" and the hope of enslaved Americans
to directly confront slaveholders.[10]

Missionary slave traders, fearing that revolt could be
staged by enslaved peoples, outlawed the singing of songs
like "Go Down Moses" and produced edited Bibles to
explain White Christianity to those whom they trafficked.
They intended to ensure that enslaved people would remain

---

[10]Saville explains that "conjure" is a framework operative in the practices, writing, storytelling, and preaching of African Americans which called
upon and related to the unseen powers of the spirits. Alphonso Saville, *The
Gospel of John Marrant: Conjuring Christianity in the Black Atlantic* (Durham, NC: Duke University Press, 2024), 10.

obedient and to limit access to stories that convey God's vision for freedom and equality. *The Slave Bible*, printed in London in 1807, included only 90 percent of the Hebrew Bible and 50 percent of the Christian scriptures. The first nineteen chapters of Exodus were chief among the list of stories to exclude. A standard Protestant Bible includes 1,189 chapters, whereas the *Slave Bible* contained just 232.[11]

Northerners and Southerners appealed to Exodus in differing ways during and after the US Civil War. Henry Timrod, who gained his reputation as a poet during the years of the Confederacy, reflected on God's liberation of the South from Northern aggression in "Ethnogenesis," which he wrote in 1861, during the First Southern Congress in Montgomery, Alabama.

> To doubt the end were want of trust in God,
> Who, if He has decreed
> That we must pass a redder sea
> Than that which rang to Miriam's holy glee,
> Will surely raise at need
> A Moses with his rod!

Leander Ker wrote "Our Happy Land of Canaan" in 1862 for White Southerners and Confederate soldiers to sing as they headed into the Civil War.[12] Some pastors, such as the Presbyterian minister Benjamin Morgan Palmer, joined the chorus by likening Abraham Lincoln to a modern pharaoh and said that his heart hardened toward the South. Northerners cast Lincoln as a modern Moses.

After Reconstruction, thousands of African Americans

---

[11]See Ben Zehavi, "19th-Century Slave Bible That Removed Exodus Story to Repress Hope Goes on Display," *Times of Israel* online, March 29, 2019, https://www.timesofisrael.com/19th-cent-slave-bible-that-removed-exodus-story-to-repress-hope-goes-on-display/.

[12]Leader Ker, "Happy Land of Canaan," musical score, Library of Congress Digital Archives, 2024.

migrated from Southern states, primarily Louisiana, Mississippi, and Texas, to Kansas and other Western states. Black sharecroppers and farmers led this grassroots movement. One of the leaders, Benjamin "Pap" Singleton, called himself the "Moses of the Colored Exodus." Newspapers referred to migrants as the "Exodusters." A Senate committee appointed in 1888 determined that the cause of this great migration was the so-called "redemption" of the South by former Confederates who subjected Black people to a new form of slavery through the enactment of "Black codes" and other forms of political disenfranchisement, economic oppression, and terrorism.

Martin Luther King Jr. frequently mentioned Exodus in speeches that he gave during the civil rights movement. King compared the 1954 Supreme Court decision on *Brown v. Board of Education* to the parting of the Red Sea. On the night before his assassination, King preached a sermon titled "I See the Promised Land" at the Mason Temple in Memphis, Tennessee. He proclaimed, "You know whenever Pharaoh wanted to prolong the period of slavery in Egypt, he had a favorite, favorite formula for doing it. . . . He kept the slaves fighting among themselves. But whenever slaves get together . . . that's the beginning of getting out of slavery."[13] King urged the 1,300 striking garbage workers and their supporters to keep their eyes focused on the issue of injustice and to maintain unity. Other civil rights' activists such as Malcolm X described White America as "a modern House of Bondage" in 1963 and identified the new Moses as Elijah Muhammad, the leader of the Nation of Islam. Less than a year after his speech, Malcolm X turned toward a more orthodox understanding of Islam, disavowed his

---

[13]Martin Luther King Jr., "I See the Promised Land," in *A Testament of Hope: The Essential Writings and Speeches of Martin Luther King, Jr.*, ed. James Washington (San Francisco: HarperSanFrancisco, 1986), 281.

support for Elijah Muhammad, but maintained his critique of the United States as a House of Bondage.

In 2014 Keeanga-Yamahtta Taylor, a professor of African American studies at Princeton University, reminded us that "the Black experience unravels what we are supposed to know to be true about America itself—the land of milk and honey, the land where hard work makes dreams come true. This mythology is not benign; it serves as the United States' self-declared invitation to intervene militarily and economically around the globe."[14] The contemporary Black Lives Matter movement imagines a world where Black people are defined by their freedom and ability "to thrive, experience joy," rather than by "their struggles. In pursuing liberation, we envision a future fully divested from police, prisons, and all punishment paradigms and which invests in justice, joy, and culture."[15]

There are other perspectives and examples that I could offer. The story of the departure of the Israelites from Egypt and the crossing of the Red Sea is consistently seen as a fundamental model for God's liberative activity, but you also see evidence here of how one's understanding of the meaning of God's freedom can be skewed by interpreting the story through lenses shaded by settler-colonialism and from positions of social power and privilege. When I ask my classes to read the Exodus story included at the beginning of this chapter, students routinely pause over phrases related to "the Lord tossing the Egyptians into the sea" and express their concerns about divinely sanctioned violence. Their concern about violence is well-taken, but they also too often perpetuate anti-Jewish readings of the story by generalizing about this image of "God's wrath"

---

[14] Taylor, *From #BlackLivesMatter to Black Liberation*, 25.
[15] "Our Vision," Black Lives Matter: About Black Lives Matter, 2024, https://blacklivesmatter.com/about.

as the only portrayal of God in the Hebrew Bible.

Womanist theologian Delores Williams critiqued Black liberation theologians for characterizing the Exodus "as a source validating black liberation theology's normative claim of God's liberating activity in behalf of *all* the oppressed."[16] Williams reads the story that remembers Hagar and Sarah and observes that there are people who never encounter the "experience of God's liberating power." For example, Hebrew female slaves are never given the rights of male slaves (Exodus 20:22–23:33).[17] She suggested that Black theologians must give attention to another kind of history when interpreting this story—"women's re/productive history" and resistance strategies.[18] You can also imagine how negative stereotypes of Egyptian people can be perpetuated and generalizations made concerning their history.

Articulating and valuing liberation and freedom in ways that embrace a vision of the Promised Land that no longer connects the theological idea of chosenness to specific nation-states or perpetuates patriarchy, racial hierarchies, slavery, colonization, oppression, and violence requires considering multiple voices and experiences in the story. Focusing on the migrant identity of the Israelites and the many experiences of people included in the text as well as looking at recent research done on the Highlands Settlements, a place where the Israelites potentially settled, brings to light a fresh understanding of God's liberating power on behalf of all oppressed people. There is a theological imagination and vision for authentic freedom that sees beyond violence, and conquest, and the singular memory of a particular historical event.

---

[16]Delores Williams, *Sisters in the Wilderness: The Challenge of Womanist God-Talk* (Maryknoll, NY: Orbis Books, 2013), 144.

[17]Williams, *Sisters in the Wilderness*, 144.

[18]Williams, *Sisters in the Wilderness*, 144.

Searching for a New Understanding
of Freedom and Liberation in the Exodus

Kate Common, assistant professor of public and practical theology at the Methodist Theological School in Ohio, embarks on the quest to bring Christian understandings of liberation and freedom out from under the shadows of ancient empires and to decouple the Exodus story from the conquest narrative in her book *Undoing Conquest: Ancient Israel, the Bible, and the Future of Christianity*. One reason she undertakes this liberative work is the overt presence of the biblical conquest narrative "in the ideology and events of the January 6, 2021, insurrection in Washington, DC, when a group called the Jericho March organized people to protest the 2020 presidential election."[19] The rioters blew shofars to announce their pro-Trump triumphalism and to crumble the walls of corruption. Sarah Imhoff, a professor of religious studies at Indiana University, commented on the January 6 insurrection that rioters used shofars "as a tool of 'spiritual warfare' . . . to show that 'the world is moving toward the end times . . . war on earth, culminating in the battle of Armageddon, and God's participation in this final battle against evil.'"[20]

Working from a multidisciplinary perspective, Common explores two threads of interpretation. One interpretive thread connects the Exodus story with the conquest narrative in the book of Joshua and emphasizes the story as the preservation of the cultural memory and theological imagination of the ancient Israelites alone. The second

---

[19]Kate Common, *Undoing Conquest: Ancient Israel, the Bible, and the Future of Christianity* (Maryknoll, NY: Orbis Books, 2024), 1.

[20]As quoted by Sarah Posner, "Opinion: Look Who's Blowing Shofars," *Moment Magazine* online, Spring 2022, https://momentmag.com/opinion-shofars-christian-nationalism/.

thread explores the wilderness and refugee experiences of the ancient Israelites, including how they define their identity beyond enslavement as they shift toward sedentary and pastoral ways of life and live in peace with other peoples. This second thread highlights how divine power symbolically overcomes the chaos that human beings create for themselves by resisting oppressive regimes and the imperial mind-set that creates systems and structures that deny the flourishing of people and forces them into subordinate positions. God travels along with the Israelites on a journey toward a new life beyond violence and bondage.

Reading Exodus through the Conquest Narrative

Common argues that Christians have traditionally read the story of Israel's departure from Egypt through the lens of the conquest narrative. Joshua, the sixth book of the Bible, chronologically ordered just after Exodus, begins as the Israelites enter Canaan, the Promised Land. God calls Joshua, son of Nun, to lead the people after Moses's death and commands him to go forth and possess the land.

> *"Christians have traditionally read the story of Israel's departure from Egypt through the lens of the conquest in narrative."*

I am giving you every place where you set foot, exactly as I promised Moses. Your territory will stretch from the desert and the Lebanon as far as the great Euphrates River, including all Hittite land, up to the Mediterranean Sea on the west. No one will be able to stand up against you during your lifetime. I will be with you in the same way I was with Moses. I won't desert you or leave you. Be brave and strong, because you are the one who will help this people take possession of the land, which I pledged to give to their ancestors. (Joshua 1:3–6)

Joshua orders the people's officers to bring them together to cross the Jordan and sends spies to check on the fortification of the city of Jericho. Once they return, Joshua and his army depart to take Jericho. The commander of the "Lord's heavenly force" declares the site of their rally point before battle as sacred ground (see Joshua 5:15). They march around the city for seven days, blowing shofars. On the seventh day, "The people shouted. They blew the trumpets. As soon as the people heard the trumpet blast, they shouted a loud war cry. Then the wall collapsed. The people went up against the city, attacking straight ahead. They captured the city. Without mercy, they wiped out everything in the city as something reserved for God—man and woman, young and old, cattle, sheep, and donkeys" (Joshua 6:20–21). Joshua is seen as a text of terror by many biblical scholars and theologians today because of its influence on Jewish and Christian self-understanding and the connection the story makes between God's liberation and conquest within the Promised Land.

However, the conquest story in Joshua is recorded from the perspective of Deuteronomist history much later than stories included in Exodus and the settlement of the Israelites in the highlands, nearly five hundred years later.[21] At the time that Joshua's story was recorded, the Assyrian Empire had conquered the Northern Kingdom of Israel, and a flood of refugees migrated into the Southern Kingdom of Judah. Jerusalem, within the Southern Kingdom, became an important exporter of crops such as olive oil and luxury goods. Josiah, king of the Southern Kingdom,

---

[21]See L. Daniel Hawk, "The Truth about Conquest: Joshua as History, Narrative, and Scripture," *Interpretation: A Journal of Bible and Theology* 66, no. 2 (March 13, 2012): 129–140.

instituted religious and social reforms, and biblical scholars suggest that he worked along with other wealthy people to increase the kingdom's social and political stature with Assyria. To do so, Judean Deuteronomists recast their history as a military victory, the Israelites triumphant in battle and conquerors of many lands. At the same time, there is also another perspective that emerges that is anti-hierarchical and anti-imperial.

An Anti-Hierarchic Movement with a Peaceful, Pastoral Identity

Recent archaeological research contradicts the association of liberation and freedom with the annihilation of other peoples and forced displacement from their land. A series of extensive archaeological explorations done in the Samarian Hills occurred throughout the 1970s and 1980s. In light of this research, archaeologists began to apply a critical eye toward the biblical narrative, reconstructing a scientifically grounded understanding of the social and political identity of pre- and early monarchic Israel.

Today, archaeologists suggest that the collapse of the Egyptian Empire was primarily caused by climate change. Many people were forced to migrate to escape enslavement, poverty, famine, other forms of oppression, and environmental crises. Common says that "people who fled urban areas were described as 'habiru' or "'fugitive.'"[22] The word "began to appear in Sumerian, Akkadian, Egyptian, and other ancient Near Eastern texts during the second millennium BCE."[23] In these texts, the term referred to "rebels, raiders, soldiers, mercenaries, slaves, outlaws, vagrants,

---

[22]Common, *Undoing Conquest*, 30.
[23]Common, *Undoing Conquest*, 30.

or individuals on the margins of society."[24] Over time, the meaning of the term changed from "fugitive" to "enemy" or "outlaw" and "morphed into Hebrew."[25]

Different frameworks have been developed by biblical scholars and archaeologists for understanding the emergence and formation of the Israelites as an ethnic group within the land of Canaan. Historically, Canaan could have been within the bounds of the Egyptian Empire. One of the most widely accepted frameworks is known as the "Indigenous origins theory." According to this theory, Indigenous Canaanites gradually withdrew from urban city-states and eventually formed the settlements in the surrounding highlands, hence "Highland Settlement." These urban refugees migrated to the highlands and settled with other groups, including habiru and shasku.

A groundbreaking study done by Israel Finkelstein, an Israeli archaeologist and head of the School of Archaeology and Maritime Cultures at the University of Haifa, suggests that the Hebrews or Israelites settled in the Highlands. The Highlands Settlements resulted primarily from "socioeconomic shifts toward more sedentary and pastoral ways of life, in accordance with political, economic, and social transformations."[26] Additionally, Finkelstein makes use of the work of other scholars to distinguish between the politics and practices of highlanders versus lowlanders rather than focusing on sociological categories of Israelite versus Canaanite. Highland Settlers defined their identities through kinship ties that were established and elaborated upon in political and social structures.

Houses in the Highland Settlement were arranged in a

---

[24]Common, *Undoing Conquest*, 30.

[25]Common, *Undoing Conquest*, 31.

[26]As quoted by Omer Sergi, "Israelite Identity and the Formation of the Israelite Polities in the Iron I–IIA Central Canaanite Highlands," *Die Welt des Orients* 49, no. 2 (2019): 207.

circular pattern with an outer defensive wall, similar to
Bedouin encampments. There is no evidence that the people
who lived in these encampments were warring people or
that they were fortified for any sort of militaristic battle.
Hundreds of villages were created and dealt peacefully with
the challenges of climate change. The circular formation of
the dwellings was intended to keep children and pastoral
animals safe, protecting them from predatory animals and
human intruders, but not in a militaristic way. People living there created new technologies such as ironworking
tools and terraced farming, but no evidence suggests that
they made weapons of any kind. Most of the villages were
built just out of reach of the military forces of the Egyptian
Empire, which relied heavily on horses and chariots to do
their work. A key feature of this way of telling the story is
the emergence of Israel as an anti-imperial, "anti-hierarchic
movement, socially in its formation by tribes and politically
in its opposition to the payment of tribute, military draft,
and state corvée. This means early Israel renounced the
right of outside states and empires to rule over it but also
refused to set up state structures of its own."[27]

Blending History and Theological Imagination

Biblical stories blend history with theological imagination. Torah in Hebrew is often translated as instruction or
teaching, but it also means process. According to Jewish
tradition, Torah teaching provides a path for faithful people
to return to their highest selves, a resource for guidance in
times of trouble. Creating, reading, and caring for the Torah
are sacred acts in Jewish tradition and practice. No metal
is used in the production of a Torah scroll because metal
is a resource used to create weapons of war, whereas the

------
[27]Common, *Undoing Conquest*, 240.

overarching goal of Torah scrolls is healing the brokenness of the world and embodying God's peace. Throughout the Torah, the Hebrew word for people is used only once in its singular form. This suggests that the emphasis, then, in this story is on people who are being led into and living in the Promised Land.

Exodus is not the title of this book given in Hebrew. It is *Sh'mot*, or the Book of Names. Symbolically, the names attributed to different empires, peoples, and characters mean much more than

> *"Biblical stories blend history with theological imagination. Torah in Hebrew is often translated as instruction or teaching, but it also means process."*

they appear. In Hebrew, the word for Egypt is *mizrayim*, literally meaning double straits and referring to a geographical region pressed into a canyon or space by one's enemy or oppressor. The pharaoh symbolizes much more than a single ruler of a particular empire. Pharaoh is an identity, not a name, representing an ancient worldview based on the belief that those born into power and privilege should consolidate power and be considered gods. This character could be an "array of Pharaohs [or later Caesars] whose military campaigns, vassal tributes, mass deportations, and support of the slave trade forced many [people] into . . . slavery."[28]

Empires in the ancient world acquired slaves through military conquests, tributes, and as part of business transactions. Power and how it is expressed, managed, used, and abused within a colonial context is central to the experience of the Hebrew people. Pharaoh, in the story, wields power

---

[28]Hulisani Ramantswana, "Sacred Texts Produced under the Shadow of Empires: Double Consciousness and Decolonial Options in Reading the Bible," *Old Testament Essays* 36, no. 1 (2023): 240.

over the people with an iron fist. Postcolonial theorists observe, in a classic formulation, that the moment of imperialism is also a moment of education. Imperialism—a system of economic, political, and cultural (and religious) forces that disavows borders in order to extract desirable resources and exploit an alien people—has never strayed from a field of pedagogical imperatives, or what might be called an ideology of instruction.[29] The empire instructed slaves that they were of such low birth and social status that they were not worthy of the attention of the gods.

Another character named is the Holiest One, God, who introduces Godself in the third chapter of Exodus as "I am who I am," which comes from the Hebrew verb meaning "to be or to exist." God is the very ground of all being. God, throughout the Torah, is not static, but dynamic and freely moves along with the people, living in, with, and among them, and cares deeply about their lives, feeling every moment in love, in anger, in hope that justice will be realized. Ronilso Pacheco, a Black and postcolonial theologian, says that in the Exodus story God uses God's power to intervene and disrupt centralizing, totalizing, hegemonic, and absolute power. Totalizing and absolute power can be instrumentalized to categorize and characterize people according to superficial differences such as citizenship, race, ethnicity, gender, and able-bodiedness. Unlike Pharaoh, who claims to be divine, this God claims even the slave, the one of the lowest birth.

God reveals the divine character and the nature of freedom through the actions of people who engage in life-provisioning activities, upend systems of oppression, and claim the most vulnerable as their own. Biblical scholar Gale Yee examines the story of the Egyptian midwives Shiprah

---

[29]Ramantswana, "Sacred Texts Produced under the Shadow of Empires," 250.

and Puah within the context of social power relations in ancient Egypt. The ancient Israelites lived "in an agrarian context of a high infant and maternal mortality rate, where non-elite rural families, the bulk of the population, usually lived at subsistence level."[30] Midwives were responsible for attending to women during labor and declaring the gender of the newborn child. Male children were particularly valued because of their potential to labor on farms. Yee says, "Under the structural domain of royal rule, midwives were necessary to help deal with labor shortages through their professional expertise regarding the birth of children."[31] Egyptians equated midwives with powerful and independent goddesses. Shiprah and Puah resist and subvert an unjust order given by Pharaoh to kill all the firstborn sons of the Israelites. When asked by Pharaoh why they resisted, the women responded, "Hebrew women are not like Egyptian women; they are vigorous and give birth before the midwives arrive" (Exodus 1:19). Their resistance to the pharaoh's orders and their subversion of imperial power is affirmed by God, who "was kind to the midwives and the people increased and became even more numerous" (Exodus 1:20).

It is easy to remain on the surface of the story of the Israelites' departure from Egypt and read the story through the conquest narrative as a battle between only God and a nation-state. In the ancient world, however, the sea, too, symbolized an opponent of God, or the gods, and the chaos people experienced in the world. The sea represented the forces of nature at war with gods of creation. The Canaanite god of fertility, Baal, battles against the chaotic forces

---

[30]Gale A. Yee, "Midwives in Egypt, Mesopotamia, and Ancient Israel: An Intersectional Investigation," *Biblical Theology Bulletin* 52, no. 3 (August 2022): 147.

[31]Yee, "Midwives in Egypt, Mesopotamia, and Ancient Israel," 148.

of the sea and the river. In the ancient story of the *Enuma Elish*, the Babylonian god Marduk splits the sea monster Tiamat as the initial act of creation. Powerful gods calmed the waters of chaos and breathed into the creation the spirit of life. During the Late Bronze Age, Egyptian texts began to refer to "'sea peoples' arriving in the region from across the Mediterranean and assaulting Egyptian-controlled cities for supplies."[32] The ancient mythology of the chaotic sea describes the final conflict between God and the Pharaoh at the Sea of Reeds as the symbol of imperialism and oppressive regimes.

At the end of the story, Israel sees the great work that the Lord has done to help them cross over the waters of chaos. The Promised Land that the Israelites enter is already inhabited by other people and under the tall shadows of ancient empires looming over the land. Once they make their way into the Promised Land, they must confront the greatest question—*how will they act now?*

At the heart of the Exodus story of authentic liberation is God's justice and vision for a world free from "imperialism and colonization, conquest and violence, oppression and suffering, marginalization and exclusion, superiorization, and inferiorization."[33] Entering the Promised Land is not about creating the boundaries of a particular geographical location but about forming peoples for shalom, for peace, and to heal the brokenness of the world. Remember the constant refrain throughout the first five books of the Bible:

"You shall not wrong a stranger . . . for you were strangers in the land of Egypt." (Exodus 22:20)
"You shall not oppress a stranger, for you know the soul of the stranger, for you were strangers in the

---

[32]Common, *Undoing Conquest*, 33.
[33]Common, *Undoing Conquest*, 257.

land of Egypt." (Exodus 23:9)

"The stranger who resides with you shall be to you as one of your citizens; you shall love [the stranger] as yourself, for you were strangers in the land of Egypt." (Leviticus 19:34)

> *"Entering the Promised Land is not about creating the boundaries of a particular geographical location but about forming peoples for shalom, for peace, and to heal the brokenness of the world."*

And, later, in Jesus's teachings,

"For you shall love the Lord your God with all your heart, mind, and strength, and your neighbor as yourself." (Luke 10:27)

A Contemporary Story of God's Freedom to Journey with Us

Have you seen the film *The Swimmers*? I could not help but think about the modern-day Exodus journeys happening all around the globe after doing this research. *The Swimmers* tells the story of Yusra and Sara Mardini, two Muslim women raised in war-torn Syria. Yusra grew up watching the Olympics and dreamed one day of competing as a swimmer in the world's greatest games. Her father, himself a former Olympic athlete, began training Yusra at the age of nine. Nothing compared to the sensation of diving into the water for Yusra. The world under water looked and felt different. Stopwatches held by coaches and judges measured her speed as her legs propelled her through the water hardly making a sound. She often emerged reaching her hand out to touch the wall of the swimming pool as the winner of the race.

The main obstacle to competing in the Olympics for Yusra was not her discipline, training, or ability; it was war. For several years, she and her family lived under constant threat of sniper attacks, and bombs destroyed their home in Damascus. They were forced to move in with her grandmother and survived in tight quarters for several years. Daily activities for teenagers, like going to school, visiting friends, helping with family chores, and athletic training, were dangerous ventures. After a few years of living under siege, Yusra and her sister Sara felt that the only way to keep their dreams alive was to set out on a perilous journey to seek refuge in Europe. There was no other choice. The sisters joined thousands of other people forced to flee their war-torn home. Yusra was only thirteen.

Yusra and Sara surfed the internet to map out their journey. Google and YouTube helped them navigate their way to Turkey, where they met a human smuggler who would lead them to the shore of the Aegean Sea. Fearfully, they boarded a flimsy raft with eighteen other people to cross the waters heading toward the Greek island of Lesbos. Midway through their journey, the dinghy's engine stalled, and the boat began to take on water. The only way to prevent the raft from sinking was to get out and swim.

No training prepares a person for the risk that Yusra and her sister took that night. Diving head first into the unknown waters of the Aegean meant much more to Yusra and her sister than competing for the perfect, quick stroke and reaching out for the edge of the pool to win a race. Swimming became the means of their salvation for their own lives and the lives of eighteen others.

Yusra and Sara, along with the eighteen other passengers who crossed the Aegean Sea on that dinghy, made it to the Grecian shores, but the promise of that land for them remained elusive. Instead of being met with welcome and hospitality, they were turned away. The people of Lesbos refused to provide them water or food. Having survived the sea, they were forced to continue their journey until they reached a refugee camp, where Yusra defied the odds, disciplined herself to work out within the confines of that shelter, and continued her training. Later, she became friends with a German coach who saw her potential and provided her with a place to live and to train. Her greatest desire was to compete for her beloved country, Syria, but she could not. She never chose the identity or title of Refugee, but it is still how she is known in the world. Her coach found a way for her to compete on the Refugee Olympic Team (ROT). Yusra says that swimming taught her much more than speed and how to win a race; swimming taught her patience, how to ask for help, to keep trying, and never to give up.

The refugee experience left an indelible imprint on Yusra's life. I imagine that, despite her resilience, she may feel like the attitudes, systems, and structures of the world continue to force her into a space of in-betweenness. However, her response is to live beyond violence, suffering, oppression, and imperialism and to use her freedom to create community. Today, she serves as the youngest Goodwill Ambassador for the United Nations Refugee Agency.

If we are to live in authentic freedom, we must choose to live beyond the violence, suffering, oppression, and imperialism that have characterized our definitions of "freedom." Like Yusra's and Sara's disciplined practice, we can faithfully choose to engage the Exodus story with God's vision of liberation for all. Yet removing the lenses and influence of settler colonialism and our long histories of conquest from notions of Christian freedom and liberty in the United States will require greater theological imagination than can be found in Exodus alone. The next chapter explores the influence of Paul's theology on Christian understandings of freedom and the stories of social mystics who believed that Christ set them free for something much more than the fulfillment of their individual and personal desires. They grounded their fights for freedom in social solidarity and pushed against social forces of exclusion, depersonalization, and dehumanization.

3

FREEDOM TO LIVE
IN SELF-GIVING LOVE
FOR THE SAKE OF OTHERS

The full meaning of human freedom (religious, existential, social, eschatological) can be clarified only in grappling strenuously with the "dangerous memory" of slavery.
    —M. Shawn Copeland, *Enfleshing Freedom*

Christ has set us free for freedom. Therefore, stand firm and don't submit to the bondage of slavery again. . . .
    You were called to freedom, brothers and sisters; only don't let this freedom be an opportunity to indulge your selfish impulses, but serve each other through love. All the Law has been fulfilled in a single statement: Love your neighbor as yourself. But if you bite and devour each other, be careful that you don't get eaten up by each other!
    —Galatians 5:1, 13–15

Paul—at least as Protestants have constructed him and his work—is perhaps the most appealed-to source from the Christian scriptures for notions of freedom. Furthermore, this constructed Paul has become the touchstone for what womanist social ethicist Emilie Townes calls "the cultural production of evil." Cultures produce evil by constructing "truncated narratives designed to support and perpetuate structural inequities and forms of social oppression."[1] Slaveholders claimed Paul's writings defended slavery. *The Slave Bible* included Paul's letter to the Galatians but omitted 3:28, "There is neither Jew nor Greek; there is neither slave nor free; nor is there male and female, for you are all one in Christ Jesus." Many religious leaders and Christian institutions continue to appeal to Pauline letters to establish and perpetuate racialized and gendered social hierarchies, forcing Black and Brown, female, and LGBTQIA-identified bodies into subordinate social positions. These interpretations are so prevalent that it is not enough to simply dismiss them as remnants of the past or seek to unravel them through historical critical and contextual biblical interpretation. Exploring the ground for and meaning of authentic Christian freedom requires going beyond questioning whether past interpretations of Paul's writings faithfully capture what he really intended to say. As significant and important as historical studies of Paul's writings are, we also have to grapple with the way the will to maintain social power and control distorts interpretations of Paul's writings. Read his letters through the lens of the oppressed, and consider ways people struggling for freedom embody a liberative understanding of Paul.

This chapter draws attention to biblical scholar Brigitte Kahl's innovative interpretation of Paul's letter to the Galatians and highlights the stories of theologians and religious leaders who, like Paul, lived in and led communities in crisis and embodied freedom in community. Kahl reads Paul's letter through the eyes of the vanquished. Paul was a

---

[1] Emilie Townes, *Womanist Ethics and the Cultural Production of Evil* (New York: Palgrave Macmillan, 2007), 4.

committed Jew, living and traveling in territories occupied by the Roman Empire. In that ancient context, Kahl suggests that Paul came to believe that freedom in Christ was a "universal exodus event." Belief in Jesus transformed self and society into solidarity with the Other. Paul articulates an understanding of the new creation in Christ as the transformation of imperial forces of dehumanization and de-personalization.

Dietrich Bonhoeffer, Pauli Murray, and Howard Thurman provide three examples of religious leaders who embraced this notion of authentic Christian freedom to live in self-giving love for the sake of others. They centered the body in their pursuit of freedom for all segments of the human population and the planet Earth. They discovered that finding their voice was one of the most important dimensions and expressions of freedom. Murray and Thurman opposed the use of violence as a tool for liberation. All three fought to maintain visibility and to transform social, political, and economic forces of exclusion, de-personalization, and de-humanization. They were acutely aware that misconceptions of freedom reflected deeper moral and spiritual problems. Most important, throughout their lives, they wrestled with ways to embody freedom in communities of mutuality, reciprocity, and self-giving love.

The Context for Rereading and Re-Imagining the Meaning of Freedom in Galatians

In her book *Galatians Re-Imagined,* Kahl says that Galatians is arguably the most influential Pauline letter because of the central role it plays in the theology of Protestant Reformer Martin Luther as he reflects on the meaning of law and works versus grace, justification by faith, and Christian freedom. In lectures given in 1519 and 1521, Luther emphasized the superiority of Protestant in-groups over Jews, Muslims, Catholics, and sectarians. Luther wrote, "For if the doctrine of justification is lost, the whole of Christian doctrine is lost. And those in the world who do not teach it are either Jews or Turks or Papists or sectarians."[2] Here, Luther defines Christian freedom in opposition to others. Kahl writes, "In Luther's perception, the Galatian antithesis of righteousness by law and works versus righteousness by Christ and grace obviously merge into a single universal dichotomy that splits the world into a battlefield with clearly defined hierarchical oppositions."[3]

Traditional biblical interpretation imagines Galatians as a dispute between Jewish Christians and non-Jewish Gentile Christians in which opponents of Paul propagate Jewish law and works of the law, and he argues against them. Historically, biblical scholars have assumed that Paul's polemical writing style reflects the influence of Greek philosophy. Kahl notes that Pythagoras created tables of binary opposites to explain the structure of the cosmos. The table was later used by Aristotle in his *Metaphysics* as the symbolic basis for the classification of things. Kahl says, "Within this framework, a polarity like male versus female is embedded into several other sets of hierarchical dichotomies like one versus many or good versus evil."[4] The passionate message that Paul offered about Christian freedom was then framed by and interpreted through these "dominant constructions of self and other, of identity and opposite, of ally and enemy, throughout Western civilization and war making."[5]

Since the late 1970s, biblical scholars have given significant attention to investigating the importance of Paul's identity as a Jew and a colonized apostle for interpreting his letters and the theological claims that he makes. These

---

[2]Brigitte Kahl, *Galatians Re-Imagined: Reading with the Eyes of the Vanquished* (Minneapolis: Fortress Press, 2010), 12.

[3]Kahl, *Galatians Re-Imagined*, 12.

[4]Kahl, *Galatians Re-Imagined*, 17.

[5]Kahl, *Galatians Re-Imagined*, 4.

scholars observe that Saul's conversion, as it is recorded in the book of Acts, provides a narrative that emerges as part of the early Christian movement. However, this narrative is not Paul's own account of his experiences, and the author of Acts is unknown. If Paul identified and lived as a Jew, then his original intended message and understanding of freedom is quite different from the way it was previously understood. Kahl suggests that scholars and religious leaders must go beyond these significant efforts to claim Paul's Jewishness and examine the importance of living and traveling in territories occupied by the Roman Empire. Paul never abandons the Torah or Jewish law. Rather, he rigorously embraces it and draws on Torah teachings to criticize the system of law and order imposed by the Roman Empire.

Kahl looks at icons and altars created by the Roman Empire to reconstruct the context in which Paul lived. In 189 BCE, the Romans, supported by their allies in Pergamon, defeated the Galatians. The territory they lived in stretched between western and eastern territories and up to the extreme north of the Roman-dominated world. From the Roman perspective, this territory was populated by a Celtic "counter nation," *antitopoi* of Roman law, order, and religion. The Romans relegated the Galatians/Gauls to a distinctively subordinate space in the imperial imagination. They symbolized barbarism and weakness in contrast to Roman strength, military might, and world-saving power. Ancient icons, friezes, and sculptures depicted the Galatians as failing, falling, dying, or dead. The armor and weapons of defeated peoples were cast in the coins used to pay Roman soldiers for their service.

Paul writes to a community gathered in Galatia that is traumatized by and buckling under the force and weight of the "Roman ideology of domination that derived its law and legitimacy from the triumph over the barbarian Other, the quintessential topos signifying hostile and inferior barbarian

Otherness that needs to be conquered."[6] Past interpreters of Paul's writings thought that his critique of the law was a debate between Jews and Christians. Kahl urges us to think about the law that Paul opposes as Roman imperial rule. Consider replacing Paul's use of the word "law" with "Empire" and "Roman imperial rule of law" to emphasize the point that Kahl is making. Paul writes,

> We ourselves believed in Christ Jesus so that we could be made righteous by the faithfulness of Christ and not by the works of the [Roman imperial rule of law]— because no one will be made righteous by the world of the [Empire]. . . . I died to the [Empire] . . . so that I could live for God. (Galatians 2:15b, 19)

Paul articulates an understanding of authentic Christian freedom here that is distinct from Roman law and the imperial mind-set, identifying living for God as a distinct practice of solidarity. "There is neither Jew nor Greek; there is neither slave nor free; nor is there male and female, for you are all one in Christ Jesus" (Galatians 3:28). This view of authentic Christian freedom embraces Torah teaching and disrupts castes, systems of ranking, the patriarchal ordering of the household, and inequality of rights. Paul radically commits to "the Oneness and Otherness of the God of the exodus whose 'universal singularity' . . . opposes the universal oneness of the divine Caesar," the imperial ruler, who, like Pharaoh, lords power over the people with

> *"Paul articulates an understanding of authentic Christian freedom here that is distinct from Roman law and the imperial mind-set, identifying living for God as a distinct practice of solidarity."*

---

[6]Kahl, *Galatians Re-Imagined*, 75.

an iron fist.[7] Authentic Christian freedom, according to Paul, is the freedom to become "a new human being" and to create "a truly human order."[8]

There are some compelling examples of theologians and religious leaders who embrace this understanding of Paul's idea of authentic Christian freedom as the freedom to live in self-giving love and solidarity, to become a new human being, and to create a truly human and humane society. In the pages that follow, I reflect on contributions made by Dietrich Bonhoeffer, Pauli Murray, and Howard Thurman to struggles for freedom. Bonhoeffer, Murray, and Thurman confronted injustice as they lived and led communities in times of crisis challenging constructions of self and society that created conditions where some were given particular advantages or privileges. Their stories and theologies cause us to wrestle with how we can embody freedom in self-giving love and solidarity in our own time.

Dietrich Bonhoeffer (1906–1945)

Christian freedom becomes visible as a central theme in the writings of the twentieth-century German theologian Dietrich Bonhoeffer for some obvious reasons. In the 1920s, the National Socialist Party threw into sharp relief the distinction between authentic and inauthentic freedom as they galvanized support and gained power in Germany. The 1920 Nazi Party platform included this statement of positive Christianity:

We demand the freedom of all religious confessions in the state insofar as they do not jeopardize the state's existence or conflict with the manners and moral state-

---

[7]Kahl, *Galatians Re-Imagined*, 9.
[8]Kahl, *Galatians Re-Imagined*, 269.

ments of the Germanic race. The Party as such upholds the point of view of a positive Christianity without tying itself confessionally to any one confession. It combats the Jewish materialistic spirit at home and abroad and is convinced that a permanent recovery of our people can only be achieved from within on the basis of the common good before the individual good.[9]

In 1933, the Nazis took advantage of an incident in which a Dutch militant set fire to the German parliament as an opportunity to secure the sovereignty of Aryan freedom and passed a series of restrictive policies concerning the right to assembly, freedom of speech, and freedom of the press. Additionally, they removed all restraints from police investigations.[10] The Nazis' understanding of freedom as a quality or state of being granted by their own authority was informed by their belief in racial hierarchy and an arrogant sense of the chosenness of the Aryan master race. The freedom espoused by the German Christians and the Nazi Party was imagined as a form of separateness, a clear break from and sacrifice of the other.[11]

Bonhoeffer cut his teeth as an emerging scholar of theology during Hitler's rise to power and under the Third Reich. He clearly recognized the Christian ethical crisis posed by the Nazis' racialized and nationalistic moral imagination.

---

[9]"The German Churches and the Nazi State," *The Holocaust Encyclopedia* online, United States Holocaust Memorial Museum, 2024, https://encyclopedia.ushmm.org/search?query=German+Churches+and+the+Nazi+State&languages%5B%5D=en.

[10]"Reichstag Fire Decree," *The Holocaust Encyclopedia* online, United States Holocaust Memorial Museum, 2024, https://encyclopedia.ushmm.org/search?perPage=10&query=Reichstag+Fire+Decree&languages%5B%5D=en.

[11]See Terra Rowe's discussion of freedom in Bonhoeffer's thought and Western views of freedom grounded in autonomy. Terra Rowe, "Freedom Is Not Free?: Post-humanist, Ecological Reflections on Christian Freedom and Responsibility," *Dialog: A Journal of Theology* 54, no. 1 (Spring 2015).

Early on in his career, Bonhoeffer maintained a purer conception of Christian teachings to prevent the church and Christian doctrine from being polluted by Nazi ideology.

Not every aspect of Bonhoeffer's theology is appealing in the twenty-first century. A more detailed and critical examination of feminist critiques of Bonhoeffer's conservative patriarchalism and the way in which his understanding of God's freedom in early writings reflects the colonialist moment are warranted. In a wedding sermon that he wrote in honor of Eberhard Bethge and Renate Schleicher, for example, Bonhoeffer said, "You may order your home as you like, except in one thing: the wife is subject to her husband, and the husband is to love his wife. . . . The wife's honor is to serve the husband."[12] Rachel Muers, Chair of Divinity at the University of Edinburgh, observes that this sexism is often seen as "incoherent with, or in tension with," Bonhoeffer's major theological insights, particularly his theology of sociality.[13] Additionally, Bonhoeffer's understanding of creaturely dependence on God and God's free choice to reveal Godself in Christ resonates with Karl Barth's theology. Willie James Jennings, associate professor of systematic theology and Africana studies at Yale University, argues that this concept of God's freedom "is found in the colonialist moment. . . . What is decisive here is that a creative authority, a creative regime, gets channeled through white presence."[14] But Bonhoeffer is also transformed by his experience in New York. What he learns about White supremacy and white Christianity from travel throughout the southeastern United States significantly influences his understanding of the meaning of Christian freedom.

---

[12]As quoted by Rachel Muers, "Bonhoeffer, King, and Feminism: Problems and Possibilities," in *Bonhoeffer and King: Their Legacies*, ed. Willis Jenkins and Jennifer McBride (Minneapolis: Fortress Press, 2010), 34.

[13]Muers, "Bonhoeffer, King, and Feminism," 34.

[14]Willie James Jennings, *The Christian Imagination: Theology and the Origins of Race* (New Haven, CT: Yale University Press, 2010), 60.

Ultimately, he intended to unhinge human freedom from the sovereignty of individual desires and the ends and goals of nation-states. Terra Rowe, a philosopher and theologian teaching at the University of North Texas, observes that Bonhoeffer insists upon a "social relational" understanding of the nature of being in the world in the context of authoritarianism, confusion, and conflict. He challenges earlier Enlightenment ideas of human agency founded on absolute separation between human and nature, self and other. Some of the best expressions of Bonhoeffer's understanding of freedom-for-the-sake-of-others come through his actions. Bonhoeffer consistently stood up against the abuse of power in community, allied himself to those whom the Nazi state deemed worthless and undeserving, and embodied freedom in community throughout a time of crisis.

Biographical Notes

Bonhoeffer was born in Breslau, Germany, in 1906 and moved with his large family to Berlin in 1912, where his father began teaching as a professor of neurology and psychiatry at the University of Berlin. He was drawn to the ministry at the age of sixteen and studied with the leading German theologians of his time at the storied theological schools of Tübingen and the University of Berlin. The discipline of systematic theology captured his interest. He cultivated a pastor's heart through service in churches, travel to the United States for a year to study at Union Theological Seminary in New York from 1930 to 1931, and his call to serve as the director of preaching at Finkenwalde seminary from 1935 until the Gestapo forcibly closed the school in 1937.

Social ethicist Reggie Williams emphasizes that Bonhoeffer's experience in New York, as a student at Union Theological Seminary and of the Harlem Renaissance and as a lay leader at Abyssinian Baptist Church, is a decisive turning point in his theological thought and practice of discipleship. The Black suffering he witnessed in the United States enabled him to discover Jesus in the Black freedom struggle. He traveled in the Southeast while in the United States, and, after returning to New York, he wrote to his Church Superintendent Max Diestal a critique of the Christianity of white America and that he had found "greater religiosity and originality" among African Americans. Williams writes, "The Harlem Renaissance turned New York into a theo-political space for emerging discourse on race, religion, and politics."[15] Music, poetry, and stories created by Harlem Renaissance artists gave Bonhoeffer the theological resources he needed to challenge Nazi and German Christian misconceptions of freedom. According to Williams, "The Black Christ" by Countee Cullen is the only poem Bonhoeffer specifically mentions in his writings. Cullen hauntingly captured the climate of racial violence so prevalent in the United States and lack of accountability that would resonate with what Bonhoeffer witnessed in Nazi Germany.

> God's glory and my country's shame
> And how one man who cursed Christ's name
> May never fully expiate
> That crime til at the Blessed Gate.[16]

The Image of God as Authentic Freedom

More than a year after he returned from New York, Bonhoeffer gave a series of lectures on Genesis 1–3 at the University of Berlin (1932–1933). Bonhoeffer said that free-

---

[15]Reggie Williams, "Developing a Theologia Crucis: Dietrich Bonhoeffer in the Harlem Renaissance," *Theology Today* 71, no. 1 (2014): 50.

[16]Countee Cullen, *The Black Christ and Other Poems* (New York: Harper and Brothers, 1929), 69.

dom in the Bible is not something ancient peoples have or create for themselves.[17] God the Creator gives the creation being and form as an expression of God's own freedom and to increase the power to be in relationship. He argued that God is not free from the world but freely chooses to engage creature and creation. Human beings, created in the image of God (*imago dei*), bear the likeness of the One who freely chooses to be in relationship. Creaturely freedom is not an attribute, quality, or state of being or a something that individuals obtain and possess on their own. Mirroring the image of God means that "human beings are creatures created in binding relationship to one another and to God."[18]

The story of Adam and Eve's temptation to eat the fruit of the tree of knowledge of good and evil is a metaphor for both the freedom and limitation of human beings. The fall is precisely because they desire to be like God and fail to see their own individual limits. Freedom-for-the-sake-of-others requires recognizing "*my* limit . . . to honor the otherness of another person, to refuse to treat them as an extension of myself, to refuse to control them with my own will and demand."[19] Jennifer McBride and Thomas Fabisiak say that for Bonhoeffer, "God's freedom for us is demonstrated in that first act of creation and is also the heart of the gospel message."[20] Christian freedom is not the same as the "freedom of secular modernity, namely, freedom of choice regardless of what is chosen; rather, it is the freedom that is modeled on God's freedom for humanity in becoming

---

[17]See Dietrich Bonhoeffer, *Creation and Fall: Dietrich Bonhoeffer's Works,* vol. 3 (Minneapolis: Augsburg Fortress Publishers, 2004; ebook edition of 1988 translation).

[18]Jennifer McBride and Thomas Fabisiak, "Bonhoeffer's Critique of Morality: A Theological Resource for Dismantling Mass Incarceration," in *Dietrich Bonhoeffer, Theology, and Political Resistance*, ed. Lori Brandt Hale et al. (Minneapolis: Lexington Books/Fortress Academic, 2020), 94.

[19]McBride and Fabisiak, "Bonhoeffer's Critique of Morality," 94.

[20]McBride and Fabisiak, "Bonhoeffer's Critique of Morality," 94.

human in Christ."[21] Thus, freedom is the courage to live in and embody the self-giving love of Christ and to provision for the well-being of all.

Transforming Communities

Nowhere does Bonhoeffer make this clearer than through his vision of restoring the church, involvement in communities and movements, and other actions. In 1933, Bonhoeffer went on retreat with other religious leaders in Bethel, Germany, to work on a confessional statement to counter the Reich Church's

> "Christian freedom is not the same as the 'freedom of secular modernity, namely, freedom of choice regardless of what is chosen; rather, it is the freedom that is modeled on God's freedom for umanity in becoming human in Christ.'"

support of the Nazi Party. The German Lutheran Church founded a seminary there in a settlement designed for caring for people with epilepsy and other physical impairments. People with disabilities began to be targeted by the Nazi T-4 euthanasia program at the beginning of World War II because they were seen as pollutants in the gene pool of the Aryan master race. Bonhoeffer wrote about Bethel as a community that "knocks down barriers," where people were free to be themselves and "the church that still knows what the church can be about and what it cannot be about."[22]

Bonhoeffer felt that the final draft of the Bethel Confession had been overly edited by a committee but found prophetic the clear rejection of the false understanding of the

---

[21]Clifford Green, Introduction to *Ethics* by Dietrich Bonhoeffer (Minneapolis: Fortress Press, 2005), 14.

[22]Bernd Wannenwetsch, "'My Strength Is Made Perfect in Weakness': Bonhoeffer and the War over Disabled Life," in *Disability in the Christian Tradition: A Reader*, ed. Brian Brock and John Swinton (Grand Rapids, MI: Wm. B. Eerdmans, 2012), 371.

meaning of the cross and Christian freedom. "We reject the false doctrine that the cross of Jesus Christ may be regarded as a symbol for a generalized religious or human truth, as expressed in the sentence 'the public interest before private interest.' The cross is not at all a symbol for anything" except God's authentic liberation in history.

When Bonhoeffer was called to serve at Finkenwalde in 1935, he hoped to restore the church through his ministry there. The church, for Bonhoeffer, is the community with the freedom to embody Christ's way of being and self-giving love in the world. His aim was to cultivate within himself and the students there "a life of uncompromising discipleship, following Christ according to the Sermon on the Mount."[23] Bonhoeffer emphasized in *The Cost of Discipleship* that the life of discipleship is "lived in freedom from the bondage of the self-chosen way."[24] Biblical stories speak of following Jesus's way of being in the world "by proclaiming a discipleship which will liberate [humankind] from all [human-made] dogmas, from every burden and oppression, from every anxiety and torture which afflicts [our] conscience."[25]

Political philosopher Jean Bethke Elshtain observes, "Suffice it to say that were Bonhoeffer . . . still living, [he] would be a powerful critic of the distorted notions of human freedom being enacted among us today."[26] Elshtain says that the "tendency in modernity [is] for that boundary to be set by collectivities like states as human beings are sacrificed to ends determined by others or, alternatively, to

---

[23] *London 1933–1935*, vol. 13 of *Dietrich Bonhoeffer Works*, ed. Victoria J. Barnett and Barbara Wojhoski (Minneapolis: Fortress Press, 1996), 285.

[24] Dietrich Bonhoeffer, *The Cost of Discipleship* (New York: Touchstone, 1995).

[25] Bonhoeffer, *The Cost of Discipleship*, 33.

[26] Jean Bethke Elshtain, "Political Order, Political Violence, and Ethical Limits," in *Bonhoeffer and King*, ed. Willis Jenkins and Jennifer McBride (Minneapolis: Fortress Press, 2010), 50.

be defined by the putatively sovereign self as I transform my choices into absolutes."[27] Bonhoeffer identifies the limits of human freedom in our creation in the image of God—the *imago relationis*. God's self-revelation in God's act, Jesus Christ, continues in community and binds human beings together in love. His intention was to confront and transform the abuse of power in community. These commitments led to his participation in a conspiracy to overthrow the Nazis in 1944. He was imprisoned by the Nazis, convicted, and executed in 1945.

> *"Bonhoeffer identifies the limits of human freedom in our creation in the image of God—the imago relationis."*

Anna Pauline "Pauli" Murray (1910–1985)

Pauli Murray believed in the freedom to find one's voice. She often referred to herself as America's "problem child" because of her call to confront injustices she experienced and witnessed caused by legalized racism.[28] Murray was a civil rights activist, a lawyer, a poet, and she became the first Black Episcopal priest identified as a woman. She lived with a sense of in-betweenness as a gender non-conforming person in a society that raced her body Black and gendered

---

[27] Elshtain, "Political Order, Political Violence, and Ethical Limits," 49.

[28] With respectful attention to the work of the Pauli Murray Center for History and Social Justice, I use she/her/hers pronouns when referring to Pauli Murray in this work. As they note, "Several scholars have explored Murray's personal journals and writings and examined Murray's relationship to their gender/s. Scholars have used 'he/him/his' pronouns (Simmons-Thorne), 'they/them/theirs' pronouns (Keaveney), 's/he' pronouns (Fisher), and 'she/her/hers' pronouns (Rosenberg, Cooper, Drury). This is an ongoing discussion among the Pauli Murray Center." "Pronouns, Gender, and Pauli Murray," The Pauli Murray Center for History and Social Justice online, 2024, https://www.paulimurraycenter.com/pronouns-pauli-murray.

her female. Murray knew well the power of the pen and publication, describing some of her advocacy as "confrontation by typewriter" in letters to prominent social leaders and influencers such as Eleanor Roosevelt. Anthony Pinn, Agnes Cullen Arnold Professor of Humanities and Professor of Religion at Rice University, says that she "was committed to an activist faith, a recognition that religion at its best is 'this-worldly,' committed to the application of the gospel to historical change, salvation as the transformation of societal existence."[29] Murray advocated for equal opportunity for the advancement and justice for all people, particularly those forced into legal and social second-class citizenship—sharecroppers, domestic workers, migratory workers, African Americans, Jews, Asian Americans, and other minoritized groups.

Biographical Notes

Anna Pauline Murray was born the fourth of sixth children to William Murray and Agnes Fitzgerald Murray in Baltimore, Maryland. Orphaned as a child, she moved to Durham, North Carolina, to be raised by her aunt, Pauline Fitzgerald Dame, and grandparents, Robert George and Cornelia Smith Fitzgerald. Her mother died in 1914 of a cerebral hemorrhage and her father, who suffered from depression, was hospitalized at Crownsville State, where he was murdered in 1924 by a white guard.

Her family was loving, affirming, and progressive for its time. Aunt Pauline did not have her own children and served as a school teacher in a local school. She started taking Pauli with her to school at the age of four, and Pauli

---

[29]Pauli Murray, *To Speak a Defiant Word: Sermons and Speeches on Justice and Transformation,* edited and with an introduction by Anthony Pinn (New Haven, CT: Yale University Press, 2023), 11.

absorbed everything she could. Learning to read at a young age left Pauli with a voracious appetite for knowledge. Pinn describes Murray's life as "dominated by two concerns: education and participation in religious community. School and church were extensions of her home life."[30]

Although her family and Black community were affirming and safe, Murray's life became unbearable when she came into contact with the White world. Murray grew into adulthood while Jim Crow laws dehumanized and de-personalized Black bodies in order to keep them firmly held in a subordinate place. She was from a long line of civil rights activists and described living in segregated spaces as "between two worlds" in her autobiography. Murray wrote, "Surrounding and intersecting our segregated world at many points was the world of 'the white people.' It was a confusing world to me because I was both related to white people and alienated from them."[31]

During her childhood, well-respected sociologists in some of the nation's most esteemed institutions of higher education wrote prolifically about race determining one's ability to succeed in school. Murray proved them wrong on every account. She excelled in school, as a writer, and in her chosen profession as a lawyer. She graduated from Hunter College in 1928 as one of four Black students in a predominantly white class. She applied to law school at the University of North Carolina in 1938, at a time when the institution was developing courses in race relations, but was denied acceptance because of her race. Murray received the rejection letter just after President Franklin Delano Roosevelt received an honorary degree from the institution and praised UNC's progressive identity. She began to confront

---

[30]Murray, *To Speak a Defiant Word*, 2.

[31]Pauli Murray, *Pauli Murray: The Autobiography of a Black Activist, Feminist, Lawyer, Priest, and Poet* (Knoxville: University of Tennessee Press, 1987), 31.

him by typewriter, corresponding with President Roosevelt and copying Eleanor.

The violence of American culture, segregationist policies and practices, and subjugation of Blacks forced Murray to practice peaceful nonviolent resistance and non-cooperation. In 1940, fifteen years before Rosa Parks, she and a friend traveled on a bus from New York to Durham and refused to move to the back when the vehicle crossed the Mason-Dixon line. Because they defied Jim Crow rules, local authorities threw them in jail.

These experiences only increased Murray's will to advocate for basic human rights for Black Americans. Murray applied and was admitted to Howard Law School as the only woman in her class. Her intellect and discipline earned her top grades and the prestige of being head of her class. But "Jane Crow," a term Murray coined, kept her tightly held in a double-bind, many positions and accolades withheld from her reach. The arguments Murray laid out in one of the papers she wrote at Howard were later used by male classmates in the landmark Supreme Court case *Brown v. Board of Education.*

I could record many more accomplishments. Murray earned a doctorate and won a prestigious job as the only Black and female-identified employee at a New York law firm. She published groundbreaking studies on laws of race and color across the United States and taught at the Ghana School of Law and Brandeis University. Murray co-founded the National Organization for Women (NOW), and President John F. Kennedy appointed her to serve on the President's Commission on the Status of Women (PCSW) Committee on Civil and Political Rights. She was also invited to be a consultant for the World Council of Churches meeting in Sweden. Murray clearly modeled and articulated women's right to preach and advocated for women's ordination in the Episcopal Church. Her thought laid the groundwork for so many of the rights and freedoms we enjoy today. In 1973, after the death of the love of her life and "silent partner," Murray discerned that all of the problems she worked on related to human rights and the legal advances that she made were ultimately moral and spiritual problems at heart. The trouble was the failure to identify the humanity and the common life that connects us all. She went to seminary and became an Episcopal priest. She mined her life's experiences with theological depth and acuity and articulated a clear understanding of the meaning of authentic Christian freedom.

"God's Inclusive Plan Pulling Me Forward" to Freedom

Social ethicist Christiana Peppard suggests that Murray understood herself as a writer straddling the political struggles and literary trends of the twentieth century.[32] Her poetry and sermons are places where "Murray dealt creatively with her rage at systemic injustices."[33] They incorporate deep theological and moral reflection and are overtly political. For Murray, an authentic understanding of freedom emerges from the ongoing struggle of people for whom freedom remains a longing and its realization requires taking risks. She "knew that the political is born in personal terms in the lives of individuals and disenfranchised groups. As such, the dream of freedom requires both discernment and struggle; it 'lingers on' as a pursuit ever-unfilled, yet it remains 'the test of nations' and 'quest of all our days.' "[34] In that struggle, the Ever-Present God actively

[32]Christiana Peppard, "Democracy, the Verb: Pauli Murray's Poetry as a Resource for Ongoing Freedom Struggles," *Journal of Feminist Studies in Religion* 29, no. 1 (January 1, 2013).

[33]Christiana Peppard, "Poetry, Ethics, and the Legacy of Pauli Murray," *Journal of the Society of Christian Ethics* (2010): 23.

[34]Peppard, "Democracy, the Verb," 152.

pulls people forward toward an increasingly inclusive plan.

Dark Testament and Other Poems is the only book of poetry that Murray published. She felt and witnessed to the promise of liberation that the United States "consistently and systematically failed to deliver . . . to massive numbers of the population."[35] "Dark Testament" was written in 1943 as a meditation on the Harlem race riots that were "triggered by a rumor (which turned out to be false) that a white police officer killed a [Black] soldier in an altercation over the arrest of a [Black] woman."[36] Murray walked through the area of Harlem where the riots took place and described it as a "bombed out war target."[37] The poem begins with the dream of freedom:

> Freedom is a dream
> Haunting as amber wine
> Or worlds remembered out of time.
> Not Eden's gate, but freedom
> Lures us down a trail of skulls
> Where men forever crush the dreamers—
> Never the dream.
>
> I was an Israelite walking a sea bottom,
> I was a Negro slave following the North Star,
> I was an immigrant huddled in ship's belly,
> I was a Mormon searching for a temple,
> I was a refugee closing roads to nowhere—
> Always the dream was the same—
> Always the dream was freedom.[38]

---

[35]Peppard, "Poetry, Ethics, and the Legacy of Pauli Murray," 26.

[36]Murray, *Pauli Murray: The Autobiography of a Black Activist, Feminist, Lawyer, Priest, and Poet*, 213.

[37]Murray, *Pauli Murray: The Autobiography of a Black Activist, Feminist, Lawyer, Priest, and Poet*, 213.

[38]"Pauli Murray Reads 'Dark Testament," Harvard Radcliffe Institute

The dream of freedom is always an elusive lure that is never fully realized. After completing the poem, Murray "felt as if a demon had been exorcised and a terrible fever inside me had been broken."[39] "Dark Testament" vividly recounts the disenfranchisement, de-humanization, and denial of African Americans from the middle passage to the contemporary era.

> Ours is no bedtime story children beg to hear,
> No heroes rode down the night to warn our
>   sleeping villages.
> Ours is a tale of blood streaking the Atlantic—
> Ours is a tale of charred and blackened fruit,
> Aborted harvest dropped from blazing bough,
> A tale of eagles exiled from the nest,
> Brooding and hovering on the edge of sky—
> A somber shadow on this native earth,
> Yet no faint tremor of her breast
> Eludes the circle of our hungered eye.[40]

Peppard observes that Murray's poetry is a "resource for contemporary democratic freedom struggles" as she models engaging democracy "as a debate, not a set of rules."[41]

Her sermons present a theologically rich account of the meaning of Christian freedom. Murray reflected on the meaning of freedom and liberation in the Exodus journey in a sermon delivered on Mother's Day. She writes, the Exodus "memorializes the ever-widening struggle of humanity through the ages to liberate itself from bondage to

---

(June 8, 2020), https://www.radcliffe.harvard.edu/news-and-ideas/pauli-murray-reads-dark-testament.

[39]Murray, *Pauli Murray: The Autobiography of a Black Activist, Feminist, Lawyer, Priest, and Poet*, 214.

[40]"Pauli Murray Reads 'Dark Testament."

[41]Peppard, "Poetry, Ethics, and the Legacy of Pauli Murray," 26.

ignorance and superstition and to fulfill the highest aspirations of human intellect."[42] Focusing on the subjugation of women as the oldest form of oppression, Murray lifts up Miriam as a symbol of courageous womanhood as she dared to ask: "Has the Lord only spoken to Moses? Has the Lord not spoken to us too?" (Numbers 12:1–2a). And she suggests that the greatest challenge of entering a new and more promising land is the temptation to "shrink from the implications of freedom and its responsibility,"[43] in this case, being drawn back into "patriarchal nostalgia." Murray urged the congregation to enter "a new land of freedom, where undreamed of culture and creativity might arise."[44]

Commenting on Galatians 3:25–26, Murray said that Paul conveys the full meaning of Jesus's coming and the freedom known in Christ. Jesus is "a model of what it is to be human; enabling each and every one who commits himself (or herself) to discover and realize the meaning of being human and of his/her freedom to exist for his/her fellow (humanity)."[45] God reveals our true identity and the meaning of freedom in the fullness of Jesus's humanity. Jesus lived in self-giving love and poured out love upon others even when they seemed unlovable.

On the eve of Christmas Eve in 1979, Murray elaborated on the incarnation and self-giving love embodied by Christ. Jesus lived in "extraordinary immediacy to God."[46] His entire cause was God's cause. Jesus was a social failure according to all measures of society's standards—never a member of the "religious establishment," a "wandering preacher without means of support," and arrested, tried,

---

[42]Murray, *To Speak a Defiant Word*, 114.
[43]Murray, *To Speak a Defiant Word*, 116.
[44]Murray, *To Speak a Defiant Word*, 116.
[45]Murray, *To Speak a Defiant Word*, 57.
[46]Murray, *To Speak a Defiant Word*, 52.

convicted, and sentenced to death by crucifixion.[47] But his life, death, and resurrection assure us of the freedom to know that death never has the final word. God is our future and this coming kingdom of love, "the kingdom of freedom, and liberation from sin and death . . . are the work of the risen Jesus, who is now an agent of what he once proclaimed."[48] Jesus's followers share the freedom to participate with Christ in the new creation, embody the new humanity, and live in self-giving love for the sake of others.

> *"Jesus's followers share the freedom to participate with Christ in the new creation, embody the new humanity, and live in self-giving love for the sake of others."*

For Murray, pacifism and nonviolent resistance were tools in the struggle for freedom. Black Americans were "called upon to save democracy but [given] no democratic place . . . in the fight to save it."[49] In an article co-authored with Henry Babcock, she argued that a pacifist "insists upon looking through the pages of history at the attempts to bring good ends by violence and sees that these attempts have always failed to do what they set out to do."[50] Freedom and democracy cannot be imposed "at the point of a bayonet" but must be won through the power of truth and practice of harmlessness. Embracing authentic freedom requires conversion to the principles of nonviolence. She writes, "The pacifist must use every instrument of good will and the power of truth to eliminate barriers to universal enfranchisement, so that we

---

[47]Murray, *To Speak a Defiant Word*, 52.
[48]Murray, *To Speak a Defiant Word*, 52.
[49]Pauli Murray and Henry Babcock, "An Alternative Weapon," *South Today* (Winter 1942–43): 54.
[50]Murray and Babcock, "An Alternative Weapon," 55.

may have truly representative government."[51] Anthony Pinn notes the influence of Gandhi and Martin Luther King Jr. on Murray's pacifism and observes that her commitments extended beyond them. Feminist sensibilities also shaped her commitment to nonviolence.

Howard Thurman (1899–1981)

With Pauli Murray, Howard Thurman shared commitments to Gandhian nonviolence and the sense of moral and spiritual urgency to humanize and restore "the category of persons" to US society. Thurman led and inspired the vibrant core of the civil rights movement as both a spiritual guide and theoretician. Martin Luther King Jr. often carried with him a copy of Thurman's *Jesus and the Disinherited*, a book that underscores the message of Jesus for people with their "backs against the wall." Thurman was what I call a social mystic. For him, the depth of one's person in connection with God was manifest in the spiritual experience, which led to an awareness of the essential relatedness of all things and one's responsibility to participate in the social process and to fight evil.

Biographical Notes

Thurman was born in Daytona, Florida, in 1899, just thirty-four years after Congress passed the 13th Amendment. His home state of Florida was a place of paradox, where wealthy people vacationed or convalesced while the state remained deeply segregated on racial lines. As with many Black families in the Jim Crow South, the Thurman family was no stranger to the struggles and frustrations of the working poor. His father died when he was only seven

---

[51]Murray and Babcock, "An Alternative Weapon," 55.

years old, leaving him to be raised by his grandmother. Grandma Nancy was born enslaved, and, from her, he caught his "religious contagion."

In *Jesus and the Disinherited* (1949), he remembered stories Grandma Nancy told him.

> "During the days of slavery," she said, "the master's minister would occasionally hold services for the slaves. . . . Always the white minister used as his text something from Paul. At least three or four times a year he used as a text: 'Slaves, be obedient to them that are your masters, as unto Christ.' Then he would go on to show how it was God's will that we were slaves, and how, if we were good and happy slaves, God would bless us. I promised my Maker that if I ever learned to read and if freedom ever came, I would not read that part of the Bible."[52]

Grandma Nancy's steadfastness, the memory of surviving as a slave, and deep religious faith profoundly influenced Howard's early views of religion.

Thurman earned his high school diploma at Florida Baptist Academy and went on to Morehouse College, where he graduated as valedictorian. He studied at Columbia University and then earned a bachelor of divinity degree from Colgate-Rochester Theological Seminary, the intellectual hub of the social gospel movement. Thurman's philosophy and approach to life developed over time and stressed activism rooted in faith, guided by the spirit, and maintained in peace. His intellectual and religious framework for social change incorporated ideas from the political left, the Black intelligentsia, the social gospel, neo-orthodoxy, and Jeffer-

---

[52]Howard Thurman, *Jesus and the Disinherited* (Boston: Beacon Press, 1996; reprint, 1949 edition), 20.

sonian democratic ideas as well as "visceral" insights from India about race and imperialism. He wrote, "The basic fact is that Christianity, as it was born in the mind of [Jesus the] Jewish teacher and thinker, appears as a technique of survival for the oppressed."[53] Jesus stands, side by side, with those who have "their backs against the wall."[54] The basic goal of Jesus's life is to help the disinherited of the world change from within so that they carve out their own space of belonging and are empowered to survive in the face of oppression.

Thurman taught at some of the most esteemed historically Black colleges, Morehouse and Spelman in Atlanta, Georgia, and Howard University in Washington, DC. As the nation's capital, Washington was the center of the civil rights movement in the 1940s. Pauli Murray encountered Thurman while he was teaching in the department of religion there. While at Howard, he and his wife, Sue Bailey Thurman, who was also an accomplished teacher and scholar, led the first African American delegation to India, Ceylon, and Burma, where they learned Gandhi's philosophy of *satyagraha* and the practice of *ahimsa*. Gandhi believed in holding on to truth to resist the violence of evil and advocated for people struggling for freedom to commit themselves to nonviolent protest. The pacifist and activist A. J. Muste of the Fellowship of Reconciliation asked Thurman to recommend a student from Howard to establish and co-pastor the first interracial and interfaith church in the United States. In 1944, Thurman accepted the call himself and co-founded what became the Church for the Fellowship of All Peoples. He was appointed the first African American dean of an institution of higher education at Boston University, becoming the dean of Marsh Chapel in 1953. Throughout

---

[53]Thurman, *Jesus and the Disinherited*, 18.
[54]Thurman, *Jesus and the Disinherited*, xix.

his career, he served as the spiritual guide to prominent civil rights leaders such as Mary McLeod Bethune, Nannie Helen Burroughs, W. E. B. Du Bois, Martin Luther King Jr., and A. Philip Randolph.

A Social Mystic

Historian and pastor Vincent Harding says that Thurman's spirituality was grounded in the beauty and terror of the embodied Black experience. Twenty-three years of his life were spent in Florida and Georgia, leaving scars deep in his spirit and rendering him "terribly sensitive to the churning abyss separating white from black."[55] Thurman never felt a sense of relief from the separateness of segregation or the moral climate that it created across the nation. His dignity and integrity were always besieged by White supremacy. But his belief in God propelled him forward to "transcend the walls that divide" and witness to the truth of human wholeness and essential relatedness.[56]

There are two central components to Thurman's embodied, experiential mysticism: the personal encounter with God and an individual response to that encounter. In the dynamic of encounter and response, the mystic seeks the knowledge and experience of the oneness of all life and endeavors to discover the sense of continuity within all life. For Thurman, hatred becomes a fundamental opposition to the mystic's life. Hatred begins when human contact is devoid of warmth and genuine connection, devolving into "unsympathetic understanding." That unsympathetic understanding can spread like contagion. Hatred, in his mind, could be a "great insulator, making it possible . . . to

[55]Howard Thurman, *The Luminous Darkness* (Friends United Press, 1989; reprint of Harper & Row 1965 edition), xi.

[56]Thurman, *The Luminous Darkness*, xi.

deny the existence of another or will [their] nonexistence."[57] Thurman's concern became transcending "the walls that divide and would achieve in literal fact what is experienced as literal truth: human life is one and all . . . are members one of another."[58] His introduction to a sermon on the parable of the rich young fool offers insightful reflections on the oneness of the essential relatedness of all living things.

> We are so deeply involved in each other and in others that often it is difficult to determine where we begin and the other leaves off. And perhaps in the quietness, we may sense the mystery and wonder, and the magic of our relatedness become aware, each after the pattern of his [her or their] own sensitiveness, of the emotions in our midst of the living Spirit of the living God in whom we live, and move, and ever be.[59]

Thurman's sense of mystical unity made it possible for him to experience a sense of belonging within a much larger community of living organisms. Nature's seasons and cycles were for him places of "special benediction." He embraced the ocean and the night together surrounding his "little life with a reassurance that could not be affronted by the behavior of human beings. The ocean at night gave me a sense of timelessness, of existing beyond the reach of the ebb and flow of circumstances."[60]

[57]Kipton Jensen, "Howard Thurman on the Contagion of Hatred and the Antidote of Love," @*This Point*. Accessed online, Howard Thurman on the Contagion of Hatred and the Antidote of Love | Columbia Theological Seminary (ctsnet.edu).

[58]Thurman, *The Luminous Darkness*, xi.

[59]Howard Thurman, "Parables of Jesus, Part 7: Rich Young Fool, 1951 October 28," The Howard Thurman Digital Archive, https://thurman.pitts.emory.edu/items/show/586.

[60]Howard Thurman, *With Head and Heart: The Autobiography of Howard Thurman* (New York: Harcourt and Brace, 1981), 8.

The Fundamental Difference between Liberty and Freedom

In March 1969, Thurman reflected on what his experience of freedom was like in this nation:

It is a strange freedom to be adrift in the world . . . without a sense of anchor anywhere. Always there is a need for mooring, the need for the firm grip on something that is rooted and will not give. The urge to be accountable to someone, to know that beyond the individual . . . is an answer that must be given, cannot be denied. [One's] very spirit . . . tends to panic from the desolation of going nameless up and down the streets of other's minds, where no salutation greets and no friendly recognition makes secure. It is a strange freedom.[61]

Thurman identified what he called a "fundamental difference between liberty and freedom." The English philosopher John Locke envisioned that "the purpose of the function of government is to protect private property."[62] Private property, for Locke, is more than just material possession; it included one's body, one's personhood. Thurman writes, "The philosopher insists that fundamental to this idea of the reasons of government is the deeper notion that man, that the spiritual, the middle all that is protected in the body is the thing that has to be free and equal."[63] The notion of liberty emerging out of the Enlightenment and embraced

---

[61]Howard Thurman, "Man and Social Change, Part I: Man and the Experience of Freedom, 1969 March 19," The Howard Thurman Digital Archive, https://thurman.pitts.emory.edu/items/show/53.

[62]Thurman citing Locke's *Second Treatise on Government* in "Declaration of Independence," (1951).

[63]Howard Thurman, "Declaration of Independence" (1951).

by the founding fathers establishes "those prerogatives, privileges, grants, that a particular social arrangement, social contract, makes possible for the individual who lives within the context of that contract."[64] Authentic freedom is something more than that.

Freedom means a "sense of alternative," connects to the "notion of discipline," and advances the dignity of the human spirit. Thurman says, "There is at the core of this experience, this motion, this push a very strange contradiction. Discipline."[65] Unlimited and absolute freedom is a "terrifying kind of tyranny."[66] Authentic freedom is revealed by the core of your character.

We are each called to live with the confidence that transcends discouragement and despair, connecting with others on the deepest level of our common ground—the very depth of our being. "To be known, to be called by one's name is to find one's place and hold it against all the hordes of hell"—fear, hate, and deception. Late in his life, while living and working in the predominantly White Northern society, Thurman grew into an awareness that freedom is more than being able to choose one's actions; it is the ability to choose the emotional and spiritual quality of one's reactions. "Freedom," he says, "is a quality of being. It is a quality of spirit. It is what the individual is aware of, if I may put it that way, when (one) is searching out, trying to discover what it is at last that, ultimately (one) amounts to in (one's) own sight at the place where whatever there is in me that is irreducible—what is it, ultimately, that I amount to?"[67] Freedom is experienced when one has "the sense of option"—the sense to feel and imagine alternatives

---

[64]Thurman, "Declaration of Independence."

[65]Thurman, "Declaration of Independence."

[66]Thurman, "Declaration of Independence."

[67]Thurman, "Man and Social Change, Part I: Man and the Experience of Freedom."

for oneself amid a much larger community. Freedom for others in a Christian sense, then, establishes "the grounds of the fundamental autonomy of the human spirit amid the social and physical, and natural forces by which [we are] surrounded."[68]

Closing Thoughts

The rich theological resources in this chapter can help us reflect on how a more authentic understanding of Christian freedom can transform social, political, and economic polarization. Paul articulates his understanding of Christian freedom as a "universal exodus event," creating a truly humane community amid Roman oppression. Bonhoeffer, Murray, and Thurman ground their understanding of freedom in the *imago dei* and *imago relationis* and embody freedom-in-community; freedom to be named, to belong to oneself, God, and others; freedom for the sense of option and to imagine alternatives. Freedom is about being responsible for one's actions and one's reactions. Ultimately, freedom leads one to take a deeper dive into social processes to create community—living in self-giving love for the sake of others.

> *"Unlimited and absolute freedom is a 'terrifying kind of tyranny.' Authentic freedom is revealed by the core of your character."*

Our society is becoming increasingly less religious. The next chapter takes this societal shift seriously and lays out a challenge for religious leaders and communities of faith amid today's waves of change. What is our responsibility as Christians to share liberative notions of freedom that chal-

---

[68]Thurman, "Man and Social Change, Part I: Man and the Experience of Freedom."

lenge ethical neutrality, total autonomy, and independence? What can we learn from contemporary movements for social change about embodying authentic Christianity today? Some will be concerned that religious faith can lead only to restricting personal freedom. Challenging the cultural divide through teaching, preaching, and faithful living is vitally important for transforming our social ecology to embrace visions of the freedom to live in and embrace self-giving love for others. The fourth and final chapter provides practices that can help communities and congregations embody authentic freedom on the front line of today's culture war and invites you to consider how you might incorporate these practices in your own context.

4

A UNIQUE CHALLENGE
FOR RELIGIOUS LEADERS TODAY

They say that freedom is a constant struggle,
Oh Lord we've been struggling so long.
We must be free,
We must be free.
—Roberta Slavitt

On the Sabbath we went outside the city gate to
the river, where we expected to find a place of
prayer. We sat down and began to speak to the
women who had gathered there. One of those
listening was a woman from the city of Thyatira
named Lydia, a dealer in purple cloth. She was
a worshiper of God. The Lord opened her heart
to respond to Paul's message. When she and the
members of her household were baptized, she
invited us to her home. "If you consider me a
believer in the Lord," she said, "come and stay
at my house." And she persuaded us.
—Acts 16:13–15

Religious and political leaders are paying a great deal of
attention to the politics of division in US society and how

it affects local communities, including churches. Some religious leaders suggest that churches should approach this moment by focusing on the biblical text and the inward spiritual journey, retreating from controversial political topics within congregations. The concept of the "purple church" has grown in popularity and is used as a metaphor to identify the blending and harmonizing of a congregation's membership which is composed of both left-leaning Democrats (blue) and right-leaning Republicans (red). For some, the idea of the purple church suggests that congregations should avoid alienating members by engaging in controversial dialogues so that they can maintain civil peace.

Students serving in congregations frequently come to me for counsel asking how to address political polarization in a purple church. Admittedly, I have never served as an installed pastor of a local congregation. I visit churches for a short period of time when I am asked to speak on matters of faith and public life. I have the luxury of talking about controversial issues without the responsibility to follow up on how the discussions may later affect the life of the community. However, I think that prioritizing an uneasy civil peace over justice and the common good allows the partisan divide in our nation to define the churches' mission. Additionally, trying to avoid conflict will neither advance dialogue, nurture a more meaningful common life together, nor deepen our understanding of the nature and meaning of freedom.

Politeness and civility can be used as tools to maintain order in White supremacist social, political, and ecclesial structures. Avoiding healthy dialogue on controversial political issues tends to marginalize and obscure the voices and contributions made to struggles for freedom by those forced into spaces of political liminality in our society and who are inspired by their faith to advocate for change. Most important, Jesus never shied away from conflict. Rather, he modeled a way of responding to political and religious tension that engaged conflict and embodied an alternative social vision. Do you remember this story?

> On reaching Jerusalem, Jesus entered the temple courts and began driving out those who were buying and selling there. He overturned the tables of the money changers and the benches of those selling doves, and would not allow anyone to carry merchandise through the temple courts. And as he taught them, he said, "Is it not written: 'My house will be called a house of prayer for all nations'?" (Mark 11:15–18a)

Ellen Ott Marshall, professor of Christian ethics and conflict transformation at Candler School of Theology, observes that "we cannot choose whether or not to be in conflict, nor can we choose whether conflict affects the human communities in which we live, we can choose how to respond to conflict and what kind of change to bring about."[1] Marshall makes the bold claim that "to be Christian is to be in conflict. Christ calls his followers into conflict with their most intimate relations, with cultural practices, with religious and political authorities, with their own inclinations, desires, and prejudices, and ultimately with the principalities and powers of life."[2]

For me, purple is much more than a blending of right-leaning red and left-leaning blue political partisanship, it is the liturgical color for the seasons of Advent and Lent in the church year. Both seasons are intended for reflection and to prepare for the birth of Christ and the resurrection that overcomes the forces of death. Rodney Sadler, associate professor of Old Testament at Union Presbyterian Seminary, suggests that the purple church in this sense should be an

---

[1]Ellen Ott Marshall, *Introduction to Christian Ethics: Conflict, Faith, and Human Life* (Louisville, KY: Westminster John Knox Press, 2018), 6.

[2]Marshall, *Introduction to Christian Ethics*, 8.

ideal toward which all churches strive.[3] A purple church does not retreat from political ideologies of the larger world. Instead, a purple church reflects deeply on political and social tensions, invests in relationships, enters into dialogue with authenticity, seeks the truth, and engages in the struggle for freedom. Challenging the cultural divide through teaching, preaching, and embodying self-giving love for the sake of others can transform social ecologies characterized by separateness, White supremacy, and the notion that freedom is a state of being that can be possessed by individuals with little or no consideration for the many who remain in bondage.

> *"A purple church reflects deeply on political and social tensions, invests in relationships, enters into dialogue with authenticity, seeks the truth, and engages in the struggle for freedom."*

This chapter explores five practices that invite us to imagine and embrace authentic Christian freedom at this transformative moment in the life of the churches and the nation—complicating freedom, creating new rituals, learning from solidarity protest movements, poetic storytelling, and staying in relationship.

Complicating Freedom

US culture and many Christian congregations celebrate freedom as a cherished American value by displaying the flag in the sanctuary, honoring people serving in the military on or around July 4th—sometimes by sponsoring Freedom Sundays—remembering fallen service members on Memorial Day, and giving special privileges to service members who

---

[3]Reading group discussion, July 25, 2024.

"fight for our freedom." In the southeastern United States, three states continue to honor an officially designated Confederate Memorial Day—Alabama, Mississippi, and South Carolina. Other states celebrate Confederate Memorial Day in some way but not as an officially designated holiday, including Texas and Tennessee. Pastors of Presbyterian congregations in the Southeast tell me stories about being asked in interviews about whether or not they will be willing to honor the Confederate dead if they are called to serve the congregation. It would be impossible for me to introduce practices to encourage deeper reflection and dialogue about the meaning of authentic Christian freedom in our society without complicating the popular and widespread association of freedom in our culture with service in the US military.

I want to approach this aspect of the conversation with some sensitivity. I believe that pacifism is what Jesus calls us to do. Jesus taught, "Blessed are the peacemakers." My own denomination is a "Just War" church. At this moment in history, the Just War Theory is primarily used reactively rather than proactively. However, I am also well aware that the military is a complicated space. Many people join the military out of the poverty draft. Uncle Butch, my mother's brother, was an unruly teenager and a frustrated high school student. A judge gave him two options to resolve his situation—juvenile detention or military service. He gained the skills to become an auto mechanic as a result of his military service. I have also taught many students who were able to attend college only because of the G.I. Bill. Additionally, the US economy is so heavily invested in the military and armaments that, if we fully divested, the economy would come to a grinding halt. I personally benefit from the investment of the nation in war and militarism even though I choose not to invest in weapons or join the military. Jennifer McBride and Thomas Fabisiak helped me to underscore this point in the first chapter as they called attention to the fact that we are all immersed in and formed by the same cultural ethos.

There really are no innocent bystanders, even when we have the financial or vocational means to distance ourselves from the military or criminal justice system.

So many of the practices within congregations continue to reenact and ritualize the conquest narrative by perpetuating the popular, widespread, and almost exclusive association of the meaning of freedom in our culture with the activities of the US military. Removing the American flag from the church sanctuary is one common response religious leaders make to challenge this framing of debates about freedom and nationalism, and instead emphasize the distinctive nature of Christian community. Although this is an important step, and, for some, a radical one, inviting more nuanced reflection on freedom requires much more careful action, such as lifting up thoughtful questions about who or what secures our freedom and moving beyond the military/pacifist binary. The military cannot be the only one to define the meaning and value of freedom in our society. Providing the opportunity to reflect on the role that elected officials, peacemakers, teachers, first responders, health care professionals, and other professions play in defining the nature of freedom expands the discussion. Also, liberal and progressive Christians can no longer view pacifists as the only ones to articulate a clear notion of authentic Christian freedom.

> "Providing the opportunity to reflect on the role that elected officials, peace-makers, teachers, first responders, health care professionals, and other professions play in defining the nature of freedom expands the discussion."

Drawing on the experience of military service can play a role in this transformative change. Bren Bishop, a Presbyterian minister and retired military chaplain, speaks about the trauma felt by soldiers who have gone to war. Bishop complicated my understanding of the meaning of freedom for soldiers who have served in combat. It is customary to welcome soldiers home by saying, "Thank you for your service." Bishop observes that many soldiers wrestle with moral injury, which makes this greeting difficult to hear. He urges people to simply say, "I'm glad you are home."

Joshua Morris, assistant professor of pastoral care at Union Presbyterian Seminary and a military chaplain, says, "Civilians can exacerbate [morally injurious events] and re-traumatize returning veterans through our collective inability to reckon with and process society's role in war."[4] War is an emotional, spiritual, physical, and intellectual experience that forms people in a distinctive way. Continuing to perpetuate "the dominant ideology of mythologizing the military service member maintains a fantasy that any conflict in which the United States is engaged *is* moral."[5] In reality, service members embody a wide variety of responses to the experience of engaging in combat. Bishop cites the story of the centurion in Matthew 8 as he appeals to Jesus to help heal a person in distress. "Lord, I don't deserve to have you come under my roof" (Matthew 8:8).

One example to consider is that, for many members of the military, the flag is not always seen as a symbol of freedom, but rather as a pall used to cover caskets in funerals and carefully folded as a remembrance for families. How does this challenge us to think about what freedom means in the lives of people experiencing moral injury and living with the trauma caused by war? What stories can service members share that confront the myth of redemptive violence? The film *Soldiers of Conscience* (2007) follows the stories of military service personnel who reexamined their notions of US American identity, beliefs about war, and found freedom

---

[4]Joshua Morris, *Moral Injury among Veterans: From Thank You for Your Service to a Liberative Solidarity* (Lanham, MD: Lexington Books, 2021), 2.

[5]Morris, *Moral Injury among Veterans*, 2.

by becoming conscientious objectors. Their stories offer a powerful analysis of the way the dominant US culture teaches us to define freedom and their experiences provide a critical counternarrative.

Creating New Rituals

Kate Common points out that "churches already possess a system for incorporating new material into [their] communal life."[6] Liturgies and rituals cultivate theological imagination, help people visualize that the world could be different, and enable participants to practice alternative ways of living. The passing of the peace is an example. Common suggests taking a creative approach by launching a new liturgical season in the church year that incorporates the Highlands Settlements story into weekly liturgy. Remember, archaeologists and biblical scholars are investigating the significance of the highlands as the place where the ancient Israelites settled in peaceful community after the exodus journey. "The Season of Origins" is a four-week liturgical cycle designed as "a yearly opportunity to focus on the work of undoing conquest, to facilitate healing the wounds of the past, to imagine the change we need for the challenges of the present moment and to integrate the Highlands Settlements story into the Christian tradition."[7]

Reverend Helms Jarrell, co-founder of the QC Family Tree, a faith-based nonprofit community in West Charlotte, North Carolina, with her husband, Greg, also suggests liturgical direct action. Their ministry is deeply involved in the struggle for freedom in Enderly Park and empowers "residents to combat the effects of systemic racism and gentrification." On or near July 4th, QC Family Tree hosts

---

[6]Kate Common, *Undoing Conquest: Ancient Israel, the Bible, and the Future of Christianity* (Maryknoll, NY: Orbis Books, 2024), 139.

[7]Common, *Undoing Conquest*, 143.

a Funeral for the Empire. The ritual is an invitation for participants to bury oppression by practicing "abundance, freedom, and common good."

Helms Jarrell writes, "I was also wrestling with internal and communal struggle over the deeply painful experiences of oppression and injustice in the United States and in our world. These conversations led to thoughts on authenticity, solidarity, expressing communal grief, and proclaiming that 'another world is possible!' "[8] The Funeral for the Empire is inspired by Palm Sunday and Jesus's triumphal entry into Jerusalem. Involving the whole community in the planning is essential. The experience includes visual art, music, poetry, participatory reflection, food, and spoken word. It is a service of collective healing from oppressive entities, including big pharma, poverty, racial injustice, gentrification, and religious institutions. Through ritual, word, and actions, participants symbolically bury these forms of oppression.

Jarrell describes how the ritual has evolved over three years. The first year, QC Family Tree held the Funeral for the Empire in a neighborhood. Artists created collages of different characters symbolically representing Empire, including Big Pharma, Corporate Slavery, White Jesus, Capitalism, Pollution, Gun Violence, and Nationalism. On the day of the ritual, participants entered the space to pay respects to the "family of the empire." They viewed the collages and listened to songs of freedom and justice. A casket was positioned in the center of the space. Organizers chose a toilet covered in gold and jewels for the casket. "What does the empire leave in its wake?" was inscribed on the casket. Ribbons and markers were placed nearby so that participants could respond to the question, scrawling their answers on

---

[8]Helms Jarrell, "What the Funeral for the Empire Taught Me about Organizing for Liturgical Direct Action," *Helms Jarrell: Artist, Change Agent, Pastor, Communitarian* Blog Post, July 13, 2022, https://www.helmsjarrell.com/blog.

the ribbons and tying them onto the casket. People ripped up the collages and put them into a casket, burying them in a tomb so that they would never come out again. Poetry was read throughout the ritual—Maya Angelou, Langston Hughes, Angelia James. At the end, the casket was turned into a communion table to create space for a feast. The second and third years, the community decided to bring the ritual out into public view by moving it to different neighborhoods in Charlotte that are seen as epicenters of greed and exploitation.[9]

Learning from Solidarity Protest Movements

One of my first impulses as a theologian was to frame this chapter as an inventory of ways churches witness to authentic Christian freedom. As I reviewed my experiences amid the current context of political polarization, I thought about the opportunity faith communities, particularly predominantly White Christian communities, have to learn from solidarity protest movements. My hometown of Louisville, Kentucky, has a long history of interfaith and ecumenical collaboration. Since 2016, local religious leaders have been called upon by leaders of several solidarity protest movements to support citywide collective action on several occasions. Participation in these demonstrations led to new understandings of how churches, as the body of Christ in the world, can embody the freedom to live in self-giving love for the sake of others. Here, I offer two illustrations.

Two ministries, Catholic Charities and Kentucky Refugee Ministries, do wonderful work in the city, welcoming refugees and asylees and connecting a network of churches and other organizations. These immigrants enrich the local com-

---

[9]Helms Jarrell, Co-founder of QC Family Tree and Organizing Pastor of Beloved Community Church. Phone interview by Elizabeth Hinson-Hasty, October 9, 2024.

munity in a variety of ways. In the weeks following Donald Trump's election in 2016, many residents of Louisville braced themselves for the enactment of policies that would increase immigration restrictions, give greater latitude to Immigration and Customs Enforcement (ICE), tighten

> *"Participation in these demonstrations led to new understandings of how churches, as the body of Christ in the world, can embody the freedom to live in self-giving love for the sake of others."*

enforcement, escalate the deportation of undocumented people, and increase the detention of asylees. Immigrant families were terrified and tried to go about daily tasks without being noticed.

A strong interfaith and ecumenical coalition emerged and allied itself with other community organizations such as Mijente, La Casita Center, Louisville Showing Up for Racial Justice (LSURJ), and Grannies Respond. Pastors and other religious leaders called upon Spanish-speaking members of local congregations to canvass predominantly Spanish-speaking neighborhoods and share documents informing residents of their civil rights, especially the right not to open the door if an ICE officer knocked asking for entry. Calls to become a sanctuary city intensified and tensions between advocates for social justice and the mayor and metro council increased. The Salaam Network was formed to combat Islamophobia. There were many more efforts made across the city to advocate for immigration justice and fair treatment of residents.

Just before Trump signed the executive order that would ban foreign nationals from seven predominantly Muslim countries, also known as the Muslim Ban, a local community organizer for Black Lives Matter and LSURJ planned training sessions for white people in the city. Many of the participants were religious leaders, and they learned how to use unearned, embodied social privilege to shield people whose bodies were labeled illegal and were raced from potential microaggressions or violence. Chanelle Helm, a local community organizer and leader of the Black Lives Matter movement, prepared whites to participate in demonstrations or to go into Trump rallies. Helm said, "Your body can be a shield." In demonstrations, stand tall. Lock your arms. Stand in front of Black protesters. Stay on the sidewalk if you are on the street. Don't talk back when confronted or criticized. When going into Trump rallies, white protesters were told to circle around Black demonstrators because they carried less risk of being harmed.

When Trump-appointed federal judges were sent to Louisville to hear asylum cases in 2018, Occupy ICE established an encampment in front of the Federal Immigration Building and dubbed it Camp Compassion.[10] Their encampment lasted seventeen days. Protesters slept in tents on the sidewalk, their bodies surrounding the Federal Immigration Building night and day.

The KKK and a group known as the Three-Percenters planned a counterdemonstration during that time and marched up to the police blockade protecting the camp in an effort to destroy Camp Compassion. Organizers of Occupy ICE called upon an interfaith coalition of religious leaders to march into the camp so that their bodies could become a shield. Black Lives Matter organizers asked the religious leaders to wear stoles and robes so that their bodies would be recognized as religious leaders. As they marched, they sang, "I Won't Be Silent Anymore."

The year 2020 also marked significant activism. On

---

[10]Reade Levinson, Kristina Cooke, and Mica Rosenberg, "Special Report: How Trump Administration Left an Indelible Mark on U.S. Immigration Court," *Reuters* online, March 8, 2021, https://www.reuters.com/article/world/special-report-how-trump-administration-left-indelible-mark-on-us-immigration-idUSKBN2B0178/.

March 13, 2020, police fired thirty-two bullets into an apartment where Breonna Taylor and her boyfriend, Kenneth Walker, awakened too slowly from their sleep to answer the front door. Six of those shots forced Breonna to the ground. Kenneth returned fire with a single shot that hit one of the officers leading the raid, a man named Sgt. Jonathan Mattingly. Kenneth believed at that moment that they were being robbed.

After that, Kenneth lay in terror on the floor nearby, listening to bullets fly and watching red blood pool beneath Breonna's body. He called 9-1-1. Police arrested Kenneth after the raid. He didn't understand. He said as he was being arrested, "What is this about? My girlfriend's dead." You can hear a police officer's response to Kenneth's questions in a video recording taken at the scene, "There is somebody dead? . . . I don't give a f***. Keep walking." Thirty minutes tick off the clock before emergency medical technicians or police go to check on Breonna. Her body lay there on the floor, invoking the social memory of the violence of the lynching era, when bodies were put on display as reminders of White power. Kenneth described the chaos in a later interview at the police station, "I'm just panicking. . . . I'm yelling Help because she's right here bleeding and nobody's coming. I'm just confused and scared and I feel the same way now. That's it."[11]

A huge wave of demonstrations swelled throughout the city after Breonna Taylor's murder. You could feel the struggle for freedom pulsing through the city's veins. These demonstrations were part of a larger wave that occurred across the nation and around the world to protest anti-Black police violence. In Louisville, protesters walked down

---

[11]Malachy Browne, Anjali Singhvi, Natalie Reneau, and Drew Jordan, "How the Police Killed Breonna Taylor," *New York Times* online, December 28, 2020, https://www.nytimes.com/video/us/100000007348445/breonna-taylor-death-cops.html.

major parkways and roads, from downtown to some of the city's statues that were erected as Confederate monuments, symbols of White supremacy. Another camp was established at Jefferson Square, which is just across from the city's Hall of Justice. Protesters renamed it Injustice Square.

A photo was posted on Facebook, taken during one of the demonstrations, showing a line of white protesters standing tall and locking arms in front of a second line of protesters of color on the street. The post went viral. A caption below the post read, "This is a line of White people forming a barrier between Black protesters and the police. This is love. This is what you do with your privilege."[12]

Amid violence, murder, and uprisings, only one officer who was part of the raid of Breonna Taylor's home was prosecuted, Officer Brett Hankison. He was charged with wanton endangerment, not murder. Hankison blindly shot ten rounds into Taylor's apartment. Three of them pierced through the walls of her apartment and landed in another apartment, where a family was sleeping. When Hankison was put on the stand to testify during his trial, an attorney asked him if he thought he had done anything wrong. Hankison said, "Absolutely not." He lost his job but escaped conviction.

Sgt. John Mattingly, the officer whom Kenneth Walker wounded, wrote an email in September 2020 to 1,000 city employees just after the city announced a $15 million settlement with Taylor's family. He wrote, "Regardless of the outcome today or Wednesday, I know we did the legal, moral and ethical thing that night. It's sad how the good guys are demonized, and criminals are canonized." He urged other police officers to "go be the warriors you are,

[12]Cedric "Big Ced" Thornton, "White Protesters Form Human Barrier to Shield Black Protesters from Louisville Metro Police," *Black Enterprise* online, June 1, 2020, https://www.blackenterprise.com/white-protesters-form-human-barrier-to-shield-black-protesters-from-louisville-metro-police/.

but please be safe! None of these 'peaceful' protesters are worth your career or freedom."[13]

Two very different narratives of freedom unfolded across the city, and the role of faith communities emerged in response to them. Black Lives Matter activists may have been training individuals to use their bodies for protection, but I now think of this is as a communal call. The body of Christ, the church, "can be a shield" by confronting the reality that public spaces can threaten embodied differences and elevate the status of Whiteness. The body of Christ "can be a shield," creating the space for people struggling for freedom to claim the very resources that communities need to sustain life. The body of Christ "can be a shield," using its freedom to challenge segregated spaces and hold each other accountable.

> *"The body of Christ, the church, 'can be a shield.'"*

Poetic Storytelling

As a practice, storytelling is central to Christian identity. The vivid language that Pauli Murray and Howard Thurman use in their prose and poetry invites us into a world of theological and social symbolism. It doesn't just matter *that* we tell the Christian story; it matters *how* we tell stories of authentic Christian freedom. Murray and Thurman center the raced body in their theological reflections on freedom. After his experience in New York, Bonhoeffer also began to recognize how racialization reflected Western imperialism, and he began to articulate a new notion of Christian freedom. Telling the story of authentic Christian freedom

---

[13]Janelle Griffith, "Wounded Officer in Breonna Taylor Shooting: 'I Know We Did the Legal, Moral and Ethical Thing,'" NBCNews.com, September 22, 2020, https://www.nbcnews.com/news/us-news/wounded-officer-breonna-taylor-shooting-i-know-we-did-legal-n1240732.

within faith communities today requires thinking intentionally about how power circulates throughout our bodies in
every context and institution—church, school, government,
sports arenas, medical facilities, families. Whose bodies
move about freely? Which bodies remain in bondage? How
do different bodies relate to one another?

Good theology is also like poetry. Sometimes we don't
like theology because it is hard to decipher. But rather than
fully unraveling the mystery of God's freedom and love for
us, good theology pulls us toward wonder and amazement,
pushing us to see beyond ourselves. Kelly Brown Douglas,
dean emeritus of the Episcopal Divinity School and Bill
and Judith Moyers Chair in Theology at Union Theological
Seminary, writes about anamnesis in her book *Resurrection
Hope: A Future Where Black Lives Matter.* "Anamnesis" is a
Greek word for remembering or recollection. Remembering
is more than a theological
statement; it is a moral
act and has the power to
form and transform our
identities. Douglas em-
phasizes that "the notion
of anamnesis derives from
Jesus's command at what
has become known as his
Last Supper."[14] On the night that Jesus was betrayed, he
took a loaf of bread and broke it, saying, "This is my body
broken for you. . . . Do this in remembrance of me."

> "Remembering is more than
> a theological statement;
> it is a moral act and has
> the power to form
> and transform our identities."

What is Jesus teaching the disciples at the table? Memory
is fragile. The act of remembering is not just about memo-
rializing the past; it is about telling the story of who Jesus
teaches us to remember. The broken bodies of the crucified

---

[14]Kelly Brown Douglas, *Resurrection Hope: A Future Where Black Lives
Matter* (Maryknoll, NY: Orbis Books, 2021), 150.

peoples around the world and God's unconditional love for the sacredness of their bodies are at the heart of our communion and the center of our moral action.

Staying in Relationship

Authentic Christian freedom is a communal act. To advance a conversation about freedom requires overcoming social divisions by building and remaining in relationship. Paving the way to live in self-giving love calls us to nurture friendships with people across artificial but tangible lines of social, political, and economic difference.

Recently, I have been spending a lot of time in the waiting rooms of physicians' offices, when taking my father, who is now in his nineties, to much needed medical appointments. Waiting rooms are transitional spaces and offer sometimes profound opportunities to talk with people as you sit in the moments between ordinary daily activities and potentially life-changing medical decisions. Both time and social boundaries are suspended in waiting rooms. Bonding around the limitations of our bodies is made easy. You come face to face with the reality that we are all just human beings.

One man whom I met in a physician's waiting room proudly wore a leather jacket adorned with Harley-Davidson Eagle Freedom Machine patches. Freedom was literally an emblem on his heart. Other patches read, "Freedom Nothing Else Matters," "If You Don't Stand Behind Our Troops Stand in Front of Them," and "With Power Comes Freedom, With Freedom Comes Anything."

Standing at about six foot three, I felt his shadow looming over me when he turned to sit down in the seat next to mine. I couldn't guess his age. I wondered for a moment what emblems of freedom I would wear on my sleeve if I ever decide to buy a leather jacket like his. He removed his freedom baseball cap to reveal slightly thinning short gray hair and clutched the brim in his hands as he sank into the chair. He clearly had a story to tell. I was intrigued.

"How long is the wait today?" he asked.

"Hopefully, not too long," I responded and then looked down at my watch. "We've only been here about twenty minutes."

"Nobody likes to be sitting in these chairs. Today, it is a check-up on my heart, but tomorrow it'll be something else. My body has been through it."

Without pausing to let me interject, he went on to tell me some of his story. He served in the military throughout Operation Enduring Freedom. His body physically bore the tale. Injured by a roadside bomb, he lived with a metal plate in his head, walked with a limp, and confronted several other medical issues that he did not spell out in detail. He summarized his story with a mature and profound observation: "My body is firsthand witness of what happens when people stop talking to each other."

Staying in relationship and cultivating the art of being able to talk across religious, social, economic, and political differences take intentional work. I hope that, in our nation's current social atmosphere, people of faith, particularly my siblings who identify as Christians, can witness to the belief that growth, change, and a better way of living and being in the world can emerge from conflict. None of us can accomplish anything alone.

APPENDIX

Questions for Individual Reflection and Group Discussion

Introduction: The Problem of Freedom

1. How do you define freedom? What do you see as the danger of assuming that people in the United States or in other contexts share the same understanding of the meaning of freedom?
2. Have you observed the way competing definitions of freedom reflect different moral visions of the good society in US public debates? If so, when and where?
3. Research conducted by the sociologist James Davison Hunter is highlighted in this chapter. Hunter observed that the culture war reflects a realignment in the United States that is "generating significant tension and conflict. These antagonisms [are] playing out . . . at the deepest and most profound levels and not just at the level of ideology but in its public symbols, its myths, its discourse, and through the institutional structures that generate and sustain culture."[1] What

---

[1] James Davison Hunter, "The Enduring Culture War," in *Is There a Culture War?: A Dialogue on Values and American Public Life*, by James Davison Hunter, Alan Wolfe, E. J. Dionne, and Michael Cromartie (Washington, DC: Brookings Institution Press, 2006).

is your experience of the US culture war? Have you witnessed a significant realignment in US American culture? If so, in what ways? If not, what flaws do you see in Hunter's argument?

Chapter 1. Freedom amid Political Polarization

1. How does political polarization affect your local community and your church? Do you experience challenges when trying to talk with others about divisive issues across lines of religious, social, economic, and political difference? If so, how do you try to overcome these challenges?
2. What are the characteristics of White Christian nationalism? Do you see evidence of the impact of White Christian nationalism in the community in which you live? What are the essential elements of freedom as defined by White Christian nationalist groups?
3. How do more moderate and liberal Christians exercise the freedom to distance themselves from other social groups as described in this chapter? What dangers does this understanding of freedom pose?

Chapter 2. God's Freedom to Journey with Us

1. This chapter includes interpretations of the meaning of the Exodus story from the perspective of social privilege and established communities, enslaved people, Indigenous peoples, and civil rights activists. How do these different perspectives and interpretations shape competing views of freedom in the United States? Which do you find the most illuminating or challenging?
2. Reread Exodus chapters 1 and 14 and consider the variety of perspectives and experiences in the story. If

you are in a group, you might consider inviting different people to read aloud and represent Pharaoh, the Egyptian army, Shiphrah and Puah, Moses, or others or to read parts of the story antiphonally to enable you to heighten your hearing of the pluri-voiced nature of the text. How does reading the story in this way affect your discovery of the meaning of God's liberation within it?

3. Kate Common argues that decoupling one's interpretation of the Exodus story from the conquest narrative in Joshua invites a new understanding of liberation and freedom. In what ways? What historical evidence does she draw on to invite us to connect peace and the Promised Land?

4. At the end of the chapter, you read about Yusra and Sara Mardini's story. What modern-day Exodus stories come to your mind that help you imagine a world free from imperialism, colonization, violence, oppression, and suffering?

Chapter 3. Freedom to Live in Self-Giving Love for the Sake of Others

1. At the beginning of chapter 3, a reimagining of Paul's understanding of Christian freedom is introduced. For Paul, as a Jew living and traveling in territories occupied by the Roman Empire, Jesus sets his followers free to become new human beings and create a truly humane community. Take some time to reflect on how this reinterpretation of Paul's writings challenges appeals made to Paul to establish and perpetuate racialized and gendered hierarchies.

2. Dietrich Bonhoeffer, Pauli Murray, and Howard Thurman believed in the freedom to live in love for the sake of others and embodied that freedom in com-

munity. Do you think that their stories and notions of freedom have the potential to help transform the political polarization of our time? If so, in what ways?

3. The stories shared in this chapter of Pauli Murray and Howard Thurman introduce the connection between the principles of nonviolence and the struggle for freedom. Dietrich Bonhoeffer, however, participated in an assassination attempt against Hitler. Some scholars see this aspect of Bonhoeffer's activism as a moral failure. How do you connect nonviolence to freedom? Are there circumstances in which you think violence is justifiable? Why or why not?

4. Both Murray and Thurman use vivid imagery and poetic language to heighten awareness of injustice and cultivate personal and communal imagination for transformation. Consider the importance of poetry and evocative prose for democracy and the fight for freedom.

Chapter 4. A Unique Challenge for Religious Leaders Today

1. The term "purple church" is often used to describe the blending of "red" (conservative) and "blue" (liberal/ progressive) political perspectives. Some religious leaders argue that purple churches should avoid alienating members by avoiding controversial topics. This chapter emphasizes the importance of engaging conflict for the sake of transformative change. What is your understanding of the meaning and intent of the "purple church"?

2. This chapter explores five practices that invite you to imagine and embrace the freedom to live in self-giving love for the sake of others—complicating freedom, creating new rituals, learning from solidarity

protest movements, poetic storytelling, and staying in relationship. Reflect on these five practices. What other practices can you imagine that would invite a richer and more textured dialogue about the meaning of freedom in the current context of political polarization?

3. Liturgies and rituals help people envision new ways of thinking and acting in the world. Two new rituals are introduced in this chapter, Kate Common's "Season of Origins" and QC Family Tree's "Funeral for the Empire." What new rituals and liturgies can you imagine creating within your context that will invite people to practice abundance, live in self-giving love, and commit to the common good?

INDEX